The Definitive Mediterranean Diet Cookbook 2023

1500+ Days of Easy, Tasty and Quick Recipes to Satisfy Anyone. Includes a 40-Day Flexible Meal Plan for Healthy Living and Eating every day

ROSALINDA SHERMAN

Table of Contents

INTRODUCTION

The Mediterranean diet includes a variety of foods that can vary greatly between countries. However, it is generally recommended to include fish and seafood at least twice a week and focus on plant-based foods while limiting animal products. This way of eating also emphasizes social connections, regular physical activity, and enjoying life. Water is the primary beverage on the Mediterranean diet, with a small amount of red wine allowed daily (though this is optional and not recommended for those who struggle with alcohol consumption). Coffee and tea are acceptable liquids, but you should stay away from sugary beverages and fruit juices. Processed foods, white bread, crackers, ice cream, cookies and pastries, and other sugary treats should also be eliminated. If you aim for organic ingredients, you can maintain a healthy and satisfying diet following the principles of the Mediterranean way of eating.

Origin and History

The Mediterranean diet is known for its emphasis on consuming a variety of foods in moderation. It is made up of the traditional eating habits of the people living in the Mediterranean region in the 1960s, such as those in Spain, Italy, Greece, and Crete. As a result, it is not limited to any specific diet, but rather consists of various diets that may vary based on cultural or demographic factors. Among the main characteristics of the Mediterranean diet is that there are always options to choose from and plan your meals around. It is not restricted to any particular set of foods, but rather encourages a balance of different foods in moderation.

What is the Mediterranean Diet, and what does it entail?

The Mediterranean diet is a way of eating that is influenced by the cultural and dietary practices of countries nearby the Mediterranean Sea, including Italy, Greece, Crete, Spain. It is not a strict set of dietary guidelines, but rather a pattern of eating that emphasizes moderation and the consumption of fresh, whole foods such as fruits, vegetables, whole grains, legumes, and healthy fats like olive oil. Fish and seafood are also an important part of this diet, as they are readily available in the Mediterranean region. Red meat is consumed less frequently, while white meat, like chicken and turkey, is used more often. This dietary pattern has been linked to numerous health benefits, including a reduced risk of obesity, heart disease, and diabetes. Rather than focusing on what you can't eat, the Mediterranean diet encourages the consumption of nourishing, delicious foods that support overall health and wellness

Health Advantages of the Mediterranean Diet

The Mediterranean diet has been revealed to have multiple health benefits, including a longer life expectancy for those who follow it. This is due in part to the fact that it is low in fat and reduces the risk of heart disease by causing less arterial plaque accumulation (Gunnars & Link, 2021), a leading cause of death in the United States. The diet also has positive effects on brain health, including a lower risk of developing Alzheimer's disease and improved cognitive function. It may also protect against diabetes and certain types of cancer, such as liver cancer caused by fatty liver. The Mediterranean diet is characterized by its reliance on plant-based foods and moderate consumption of fish, while red meat and processed foods are limited. It also promotes social connections and daily physical activity.

An eating plan for a lifestyle

You do not have to monitor your calorie consumption while following the Mediterranean diet. It involves making lifestyle changes. Actually, the intention of this diet is to help you live a better life. As with those in the Mediterranean area, those who adhere to this diet take better care of themselves, feel better about themselves, and have healthier bodies.

There are other factors of this diet that are important besides just eating delicious food. In reality, two key aspects of Mediterranean lifestyles are frequent exercise and dining with close friends or family. Actually, all of this helps to enhance your physical, emotional, and mental health as a whole.

Because of this, it is best to describe it as a healthy lifestyle rather than merely a diet.

Additional than food, this diet consists of other elements. Following this diet encourages you to dine with your friends and family. As was previously said, it is suggested that you combine this diet with regular exercise to get the most out of it. Your physical and mental health will both significantly improve as a result.

The Mediterranean meal plan

Consume extra virgin olive oil as a condiment to add additional fat to your diet together with legumes, fruit, vegetables, and grains. Consume yoghurt and cheese sometimes in moderation. Approximately two or three times each week, consume fish and seafood. It is permissible to occasionally pair wine with meals.

Why the Mediterranean Diet is Effective?

When it comes down to it, weight loss is easy. Everything depends on how much energy you take in daily compared to how much energy you use.

If you consume 3200 calories a day but work a desk job and don't exercise, your base metabolic rate—the number of calories you need to maintain your body—will be low. Let's say for the sake of argument that your BMR at the end of the day is 2400. That means you consumed 800 calories more than you required. Despite the fact that it may not seem like much, if it happened every day for the whole week, you would have ingested 5600 more calories than were necessary to maintain your present weight.

Given that one pound equals around 3500 calories, you would likely gain one pound that week and use the remaining 2100 calories to increase your caloric intake the next week (Mayo Clinic, n.d.). If you continue to feed your body more than it needs, the weight will continue to increase. The math is straightforward.

Undoubtedly, other factors also come into play, such as your age, build, metabolism, and hormones if you're a woman.

The Mediterranean Food Pyramid

The Mediterranean Diet pyramid is a helpful guide for understanding the proportions and frequency of different types of foods to include in your diet. It includes social factors, like eating with family and participating in physical activity, as the foundation, emphasizing that the Mediterranean Diet is a lifestyle rather than just a way of eating.

The pyramid recommends consuming fruits, vegetables, grains, legumes, beans, nuts and seeds, herbs and spices, olive oil, and other healthy fats daily. It suggests limiting dairy, poultry, eggs, and fish to three to five times per week, and reserving meat, potatoes, rice, pasta, flour products, and sweets for occasional consumption.

However, it's important to note that the pyramid advises caution with simple carbohydrates like white flour and added sugars, as they can cause rapid fluctuations in blood sugar and contribute to conditions like insulin resistance and diabetes. Instead, it recommends incorporating complex carbs like whole grains and oatmeal, which break down more slowly and provide sustained feelings of fullness.

Main Ingredients of the Mediterranean Pyramid

The Mediterranean diet is more of a way of life than a strict meal plan. It emphasizes the importance of social connections, daily physical activity, and enjoying life. The diet pyramid devised by Oldways, in partnership with the World Health Organization and the Harvard School of Public Health, reflects this focus on a balanced lifestyle.

At the base of the pyramid are daily activities and social gatherings, emphasizing the importance of both healthy eating and social interactions. The next level includes the recommended daily intake of fruits, vegetables, legumes, nuts, and herbs. Fish and seafood are included in the next level, to be consumed a few times per week. The top level of the pyramid includes red meat, to be consumed sparingly, and wine and other alcoholic beverages, to be enjoyed in moderation.

The Mediterranean diet allows for a variety of delicious and nutritious foods, but emphasizes the importance of moderation in all aspects of life.

The 6 advantages of the Mediterranean diet

The Mediterranean diet can have a variety of benefits for your health, including improved brain function, weight loss, better gut health, reduced risk of cancer, improved heart health, and improved mental health.

This is due to the inclusion of nutrient-dense foods like fish, vegetables, legumes, fruits, eggs, and dairy products in the diet, as well as the high levels of omega-3 fatty acids and healthy bacteria in the gut.

In addition, the emphasis on social interaction and physical activity as part of the Mediterranean lifestyle can also contribute to overall health and well-being.

Important Foodstuffs

Vitamins: Fruits and vegetables, which are abundant in vitamins and essential for the body's correct operation, are a fundamental part of the Mediterranean diet.

Vitamin A, for example, promotes the health of your bones and teeth while also keeping your hair, nails, and skin in excellent condition. Foods that are high in vitamin A include carrots, sweet potatoes, mango, leafy greens, melon, and herring.

On the other hand, B vitamins play a crucial role in brain, nerve, and metabolism function, as well as supporting the production of red blood cells and DNA synthesis. Some Mediterranean foods that are high in vitamin B include eggs, milk, avocados, spinach, tuna, salmon, beans, almonds, and seeds.

Vitamin C, which is known for supporting the immune system and helping the body absorb iron and produce collagen, can be found in papaya, tomatoes, kale, oranges, broccoli, strawberries, and cauliflower.

Vitamin D, which is necessary for calcium absorption and bone formation, can be found in sardines, egg yolks, mushrooms, salmon, and canned tuna.

Vitamin E, which can protect the body from infections and prevent eye damage, can be found in nuts, seeds, vegetable oils, and green vegetables.

Finally, vitamin K, which supports bone health and enhances kidney, cognitive, and heart health, can be found in green leafy vegetables, eggs, kiwi, prunes, vegetable oil, and parsley.

Overall, the Mediterranean diet is a great way to ensure that you are getting all of the essential vitamins that your body requires.

Minerals — Iron, beta-carotene, potassium, sulfur, calcium, sodium, and magnesium are the minerals that are most crucial to human health. The Mediterranean diet is rich in minerals that are crucial for maintaining good health. Iron, for example, is crucial for carrying oxygen from the lungs to the rest of the body, and it can be found in foods such as beans, sardines, and dark leafy greens.

Beta-carotene is a powerful antioxidant that helps to protect cells from damage, and it is found in abundance in fruits and vegetables such as carrots, sweet potatoes, and spinach.

Potassium is an essential mineral that helps to regulate heart function, and it can be found in foods such as avocados, potatoes, and bananas.

Sulfur is important for healthy skin, hair, and nails, and it can be found in foods such as garlic, onions, and eggs.

Calcium is necessary for strong bones and teeth, and it can be found in dairy products such as milk, yogurt, and cheese.

Sodium and magnesium are also essential minerals that are found in a variety of foods, including nuts, seeds, and leafy greens.

Overall, the Mediterranean diet is an excellent source of a wide range of minerals that are necessary for optimal health.

Healthy Fats: The Mediterranean diet is rich in healthy fats, such as **monounsaturated fats** and **omega-3** fatty acids, which are beneficial for heart and brain health. These healthy fats can be found in foods like nuts, seeds, and fatty fish. However, it is important to limit consumption of unhealthy fats like saturated and trans fats, which are found in processed and fried foods. These unhealthy fats can increase the risk of heart disease and other health issues. To follow a healthy Mediterranean diet, it is important to choose foods that are high in healthy fats and low in unhealthy fats, such as olive oil, avocados, and fatty fish.

Vegetables Are a Must in Your Meals

Incorporating vegetables into your meals is a key aspect of the Mediterranean diet. Not only do vegetables provide important nutrients such as vitamins, minerals, and fiber, they also contribute to the delicious and diverse flavors of Mediterranean dishes. Some examples of vegetables commonly found in the Mediterranean diet include tomatoes, cucumbers, bell peppers, eggplants, onions, garlic, and leafy greens like spinach and kale.

These vegetables can be enjoyed raw in salads, grilled as a side dish, or added to main dishes like stews and soups. The versatility of vegetables allows for endless possibilities in the kitchen, making it easy to incorporate them into your meals on a daily basis. So why not give it a try and see how adding more vegetables to your diet can improve your overall health and well-being in the long run?

Drink a lot

Drinking water is an essential aspect of the Mediterranean diet and is crucial for maintaining optimal health and hydration. It is recommended to drink at least 8 cups of water per day to keep your body properly hydrated and functioning at its best.

In the Mediterranean diet, it is encouraged to drink water as your main source of hydration, rather than sugary drinks or juices. In addition to plain water, other hydrating options such as herbal teas and mineral water can also be included in your daily routine.

Fruits and vegetables, which are high in water content, can also help to keep your body hydrated. Some examples of hydrating fruits and vegetables to include in your diet are cucumbers, watermelon, spinach, apples, tomatoes, broccoli, and oranges. By ensuring that you are getting enough water, you can support the proper functioning of your muscles, aid in the cleansing of your body, and prevent overheating. So, it is essential to make sure you are properly hydrated as part of following a Mediterranean diet.

Mediterranean Diet in a Nutshell

The simplest method for adjusting to a Mediterranean diet is to start small. To achieve this, use olive oil for butter when sautéing food.

By snacking on fruit, eating salad as an appetizer or side dish, and incorporating vegetables into other dishes, you can increase the number of fruits and vegetables you consume.

Prefer whole grains to processed bread, rice, and pasta. Replace red meat with fish at least twice a week. Use skim or 1 percent milk instead of 2 percent or whole milk to cut back on your intake of high-fat dairy items.

How to Bring About Change

Here are some suggestions to get you started if the prospects of changing your eating practices to a Mediterranean diet makes you uneasy: eat plenty of vegetables. There should always be breakfast. Fruit, whole grains, and other foods high in fiber are great breakfast options since they will keep you full for several hours.

Eat fish twice per week. Salmon, herring, tuna, sablefish, and sardines are fish high in omega-3 fatty acids; shellfish like mussels, oysters, and clams also provide benefits for heart and brain health.

Once per week, prepare a vegetarian meal. Consider joining the "Meatless Mondays" trend by abstaining from eating meat at the beginning of your week. Alternatively, pick a day when you just eat vegetables, nutritious grains, and beans for your meals. Once you've gotten the hang of it, practice it twice a week.

Consuming dairy products in moderation is advised. The U.S. Department of Agriculture advises consuming no more saturated fat than 10% of daily calories. That implies that you may keep consuming dairy products like plain or Greek yogurt and unprocessed cheese.

Enjoy dessert with fresh fruit. Pick fresh figs, strawberries, grapes, cake, or other baked goods.

Utilize beneficial fats. Healthy fats can be found in abundance in extra-virgin olive oil, olives, almonds, sunflower seeds, and avocados.

The word "diet" connotes a strict set of guidelines to follow, such as counting calories and avoiding food groups that your body requires. Thankfully, when dining in the Mediterranean style, that is not the case. The Mediterranean diet is a plant-based diet that prioritizes lean proteins from fish and poultry as well as healthy fats from foods like extra virgin olive oil. It also emphasizes vegetables, fruits, whole grains, nuts, beans, and legumes. As indicated at the very top of the pyramid, in the Mediterranean diet red meats and sweets are consumed rarely. This is a terrific place to start if you're new to the Mediterranean diet. During the first week, purchase some premium extra virgin olive oil and start using it as your main cooking oil.

The following week, try to include 1 or 2 meals with fish or seafood and 1 or 2 vegetarian meals. Stock up on fruit or dried fruit, hummus, vegetables, and other healthy snacks and foods. As an alternative to the slice of cake, serve a modest piece of traditionally produced cheese, such as Pecorino Romano, feta, and Parmigiano-Reggiano, with a fresh fruit or a handful of dried fruit such as apricots, cherries or figs.

The Mediterranean diet is a healthy alternative to many traditional diets that focus on restriction, a positive approach to eating that emphasizes flavor and the pleasure at the table while celebrating delicious meals.

BREAKFAST

Banana Quinoa Delight

Serves: 3 **Time**: 20 Minutes

Ingredients:
3/4 cup quinoa, soaked in water for 1 hour
8 ounces almond milk, canned
3/4 cup water
1 teaspoon pure vanilla extract
1/2 cup sliced banana
A pinch of sea salt

Toppings:
6 sliced bananas
Grated chocolate (optional)

Directions: In a pressure cooker, combine the soaked quinoa, almond milk, water, vanilla extract, sliced banana, and sea salt. Secure the lid and cook on the "rice" setting for 12 minutes on low pressure. Release the pressure naturally and stir the mixture. Divide it into serving bowls and top with additional sliced bananas and grated chocolate, if desired.

Nutrition: Calories: 371, Protein: 7.3 Grams, Fat: 20.4 Grams, Carbs: 41.4 Grams, Sodium: 17.4 mg

Spinach Feta Breakfast

Prep time: 10 minutes **Cook time:** 10 minutes **Serving:** 4

Ingredients:
Large eggs, 10
Baby spinach, 1/2 pound
Wholewheat tortillas, 4
Cherry or grape tomatoes, 1/2 pint
Feta cheese crumbled 4 ounces
Butter or olive oil, as per need
Salt & pepper as per taste

Directions: Crack the eggs into a bowl and whisk them together with a fork. Heat a pan over medium heat and add a bit of butter or olive oil. Once the pan is hot, add the spinach and cook until it's wilted, about 2-3 minutes. Pour the eggs into the pan with the spinach and use a spatula to scramble them together. When the eggs are cooked to your liking, remove the pan from the heat and set it aside. Warm the tortillas in a separate pan over medium heat until they're hot and pliable. Assemble the spinach feta breakfast wraps by placing a portion of the egg and spinach mixture onto each tortilla, followed by a few cherry tomatoes and a sprinkle of feta cheese. Roll up the tortillas and enjoy!

Nutrition: Calories: 249, Fat: 16g, Protein: 16g, Carbohydrates: 15g, Fiber: 3g, Sugar: 2g, Sodium: 561mg

Ricotta, Mushroom & Egg Fried Tartine

Prep Time: 10 minutes **Cook time:** 20 minutes **Serving:** 2

Ingredients
Crusty bread, 2 slices
Olive oil, as per taste

Part skim ricotta, 1/3 cup
Butter, 2 tablespoons
Garlic, 2 cloves
Mixed mushrooms, 1 1/2 cup
Sherry vinegar, 1 tablespoon
Chopped walnuts, 1/4 cup
Eggs, 2
Calabrian chilies, 2 tablespoons
Parsley, dill and basil, for garnishing

Directions: Preheat your oven to 350°F (180°C). Slice the crusty bread into 1-inch-thick slices and brush each slice with a bit of olive oil. Place the bread slices on a baking sheet and bake them in the preheated oven for 8-10 minutes, or until they're crispy and lightly golden brown. While the bread is toasting, heat a pan over medium heat and add the butter. Once the butter is melted, add the garlic and mushrooms to the pan and cook until the mushrooms are tender, about 5-7 minutes. Add the sherry vinegar to the pan with the mushrooms and cook for an additional minute. Divide the ricotta cheese among the toasted bread slices and top each slice with a portion of the mushroom mixture. Crack an egg into each bread-and-mushroom-topped tartine and sprinkle the Calabrian chilies and chopped walnuts over the top. Place the tartines back in the oven and bake for 8-10 minutes, or until the eggs are cooked to your liking. Garnish the tartines with parsley, dill, and basil.

Nutrition per serving: Calories: 413, Fat: 26 g, Saturated fat: 10 g, Cholesterol: 173 mg, Sodium: 551 mg, Carbohydrates: 28 g, Fiber: 3 g, Protein: 17 g

Sautéed Dandelion Toast

Prep Time: 5 minutes **Cook time:** 10 minutes **Serving:** 4

Ingredients:
Olive oil, 2 tablespoons
Red onion, 1
Red pepper flakes, 1/8 tablespoon
Lemon juice, 2 tablespoons
Dandelion greens, 1 bunch
Salt, 1/4 tablespoon
Pepper, 1/4 tablespoon
Feta cheese, 4 oz.
Plain yogurt, 1/4 cup.
Grated lemon zest, 1 tablespoon
Ciabatta, 1 loaf
Small mint leaves, 2 tablespoons

Directions: Heat the olive oil in a pan over medium heat. Slice the red onion into thin wedges and add them to the pan. Cook until the onions are translucent, about 5-7 minutes. Add the red pepper flakes, lemon juice, and dandelion greens to the pan with the onions. Cook until the greens are wilted, about 2-3 minutes. Season the greens with salt and pepper, to taste. In a small bowl, mix together the feta cheese, yogurt, and lemon zest. Slice the ciabatta into 1-inch-thick slices and toast them until they're crispy and golden brown. Spread the feta cheese mixture over the toasted ciabatta slices and top each slice with a portion of the sautéed dandelion greens. Garnish with small mint leaves and serve hot.

Nutrition: Calories: 215, Fat: 12 g, Saturated fat: 5 g, Carbohydrates: 22 g, Fiber: 2 g, Protein: 7 g, Cholesterol: 28 mg, Sodium: 510 mg

Yogurt with dark chocolate flakes and almonds

Prep time: 3 min | **Cook time:** 0 min | **Servings:** 2

Ingredients
⅓ c. Vanilla Greek yogurt
2 tsp. Nature sliced almonds
2 tsps. Honey
1c. dark chocolate flakes

Directions: Scoop the vanilla Greek yogurt into a bowl. Sprinkle the sliced almonds over the top. Drizzle the honey over the almonds and yogurt. Sprinkle the dark chocolate flakes over the top.

Nutrition per serving: calories 200, Proteins 15 g, Fat 20 g, saturated fats: 10 g, Carbohydrates: 25 g, Sugars: 15 g, Fiber: 3 g, Sodium: 100 g

Warm Bulgur Breakfast Bowls with Fruits

Preparation time: 10   minutes **Cooking time:** 15 minutes **Servings:** 6

Ingredients:
2 cups unsweetened almond milk
1½ cups uncooked bulgur
2 cups water
½ teaspoon ground cinnamon
2 cups frozen (or fresh, pitted) dark sweet cherries 8 dried (or fresh) figs, chopped
½ cup chopped almonds
¼ cup loosely packed fresh mint, chopped

Directions: In a medium saucepan, bring the almond milk, water, and cinnamon to a boil. Add the bulgur to the pot and reduce the heat to a simmer. Cover the pot and cook the bulgur for 15-20 minutes, or until it's tender and all of the liquid has been absorbed. While the bulgur is cooking, heat a separate pan over medium heat and add the cherries. Cook the cherries until they're warm and starting to release their juices, about 5-7 minutes. Once the bulgur is cooked, divide it among bowls and top each bowl with the cherry mixture, chopped figs, chopped almonds, and fresh mint.

Nutrition: calories: 207, fat: 6.0g, protein: 8.0g, carbs: 32.0g, fiber: 4.0g, sodium: 82mg

Broccoli and Eggs

Serves: 4 **Time:** 40 Minutes

Ingredients:
1 Onion, Chopped
6 Eggs, Beaten
1 Tablespoon All Purpose Flour
1 lb. Broccoli, Chopped into Florets

Directions: Heat a pan over medium heat and add a bit of oil. Once the pan is hot, add the chopped onion and cook until it's translucent, about 5-7 minutes. Add the broccoli florets to the pan with the onion and cook until they're tender, about 5-7 minutes. In a bowl, whisk together the eggs and flour. Pour the egg mixture into the pan with the broccoli and onions, and use a spatula to scramble everything together. Cook the eggs until they're fully set, about 5-7 minutes. Serve hot.

Nutrition: Calories: 160, Protein: 13 Grams, Fat: 8 Grams, Carbs: 10 Grams, Sodium: 147 mg

Hazelnuts, Blueberries with Grain Salad

Prep Time: 5 minutes **Cook time:** 15 minutes **Serving:** 4

Ingredients:
1 cup steelcut oats
1 cup dry golden quinoa
1/2 cup dry millet
3 tablespoons olive oil
1/2" piece of fresh ginger, minced
1 teaspoon lemon zest
1/2 cup maple syrup
1 cup Greek yogurt
1/4 teaspoon nutmeg
2 cups roughly chopped hazelnuts
2 cups blueberries

Directions: In a pot, bring 4 cups of water to a boil. Add the steelcut oats, quinoa, and millet. Reduce the heat to low and simmer for 15-20 minutes, or until the grains are cooked. In a saucepan, heat the olive oil over medium heat. Add the minced ginger and cook for 1-2 minutes, or until fragrant. Remove the pan from the heat and stir in the lemon zest and maple syrup. In a large mixing bowl, combine the cooked grains, ginger-maple syrup mixture, Greek yogurt, and nutmeg. Stir to combine. Divide the mixture among 4 bowls and top each bowl with a handful of hazelnuts and blueberries.

Nutrition per serving: Calories: 484, Fat: 25g, Saturated fat: 3g, Cholesterol: 7mg, Sodium: 94mg, Carbohydrates: 60g, Fiber: 6g, Sugar: 25g, Protein: 13g

Breakfast Pancakes with Berry Sauce

Preparation time: 3 minutes **Cooking time:** 15 minutes **Servings:** 4

Ingredients:
Pancakes:
1 cup almond flour
1 teaspoon baking powder
¼ teaspoon salt
6 tablespoon extravirgin olive oil, divided
3 large eggs, beaten
Zest and juice of 1 lemon
½ teaspoon vanilla extract
Berry Sauce:
1 cup frozen mixed berries
1 tablespoon water, plus more as needed
½ teaspoon vanilla extract

Directions: In a mixing bowl, whisk together the almond flour, baking powder, and salt. Add 3 tablespoons of the olive oil, the beaten eggs, lemon zest and juice, and vanilla extract to the dry ingredients. Stir until well combined. Heat a griddle or large nonstick pan over medium heat. Add 1 tablespoon of olive oil to the pan. Once the pan is hot, drop ¼ cup portions of the pancake batter onto the griddle. Cook for 2-3 minutes on one side, until bubbles form on the surface and the edges start to look dry. Flip the pancakes and cook for an additional 1-2 minutes, until golden brown on both sides. Repeat this process with the remaining pancake batter, adding more olive oil to the pan as needed. While the pancakes are cooking, let's make the berry sauce. In a small saucepan, combine the frozen berries, 1 tablespoon of water, and ½ teaspoon of vanilla extract. Cook over medium heat, stirring occasionally, until the berries are thawed and the sauce has thickened. If the sauce becomes too thick, add a little more water to thin it out. Stack the pancakes on a plate and top with the berry sauce.

Nutrition: calories: 275, fat: 26.0g, protein: 4.0g, carbs: 8.0g, fiber: 2.0g, sodium: 271mg

Nectarine Bruschetta

Total Time 15 minutes **Difficulty Level** low **Servings** 2

Ingredients:
1 teaspoon honey
1 1/2 tablespoons white wine vinegar
2 slices of bread
1 sliced nectarine
2 teaspoons black pepper (coarsely crushed)
1/4 cup olive oil
1/3 cup fresh ricotta cheese

Directions: In a mixing bowl, combine the sliced nectarines, honey, white wine vinegar, and black pepper. Set this mixture aside. Heat a griddle or large skillet over medium heat and add in a drizzle of olive oil. Place the bread slices onto the griddle and toast for 2-3 minutes on each side, or until lightly golden and crispy. Once the bread is toasted, remove it from the griddle and spread a generous amount of ricotta cheese onto each slice. Top the ricotta with the nectarine mixture and then drizzle the remaining olive oil over the top. Whisk honey and white wine vinegar in a cup until completely dissolved. Toss in the nectarine and set aside to marinate for 10 minutes. Toss in olive oil and season with freshly ground black pepper. Spread ricotta on toast and top with nectarines and their juices.

Nutrition: Calories: 375, Total Fat: 27g, Saturated Fat: 9g, Cholesterol: 33mg, Sodium: 225 mg, Carbohydrates: 33g, Fiber: 2-3g, Sugar: 19g, Protein: 7g

Strawberry Thyme Millet Bowl

Preparation Time: 15 minutes **Cooking Time**: 20 minutes **Servings**: 1

Ingredients:
1 lb. strawberries, hulled and halved
4 sprigs of fresh thyme
1 1/2 tsp. pure vanilla extract
2 tbsp. finely chopped pistachios
2 tbsp. hemp seeds
1 tbsp. olive oil
1 tbsp. honey
1 cup 2% milk, plus more for serving
1 cup millet

Directions: Rinse the millet thoroughly in a fine mesh sieve and then add it to a medium saucepan with 2 cups of water. Bring the mixture to a boil, reduce the heat to low, and simmer for 20-25 minutes, or until the millet is cooked and the water is absorbed. Remove the pan from the heat and let it sit for 5 minutes before fluffing the millet with a fork. While the millet is cooking, let's make the strawberry thyme topping. In a small skillet over medium heat, add in the olive oil and the halved strawberries. Cook the strawberries for 5-7 minutes, or until they are soft and juicy. Remove the pan from the heat and stir in the thyme leaves, vanilla extract, and honey. To assemble the bowl, place a generous scoop of the cooked millet into a bowl and top it with the strawberry thyme mixture. Sprinkle the chopped pistachios and hemp seeds over the top and then drizzle a splash of milk over the bowl. Serve it up with a side of yogurt or a glass of cold milk for a delicious and healthy breakfast.

Nutrition: cal 358, pro 11 g, carb 54 g, fiber 7 g, sugars 14.5 g (added sugars4.5 g), fat 11 g (sat fat 2 g), chol 6 mg, sodium 37 mg

Scrambled Egg Tacos

Preparation Time: 15 minutes **Cooking Time:** 20 minutes **Servings:** 1

Ingredients:
2 tbsp. olive oil, divided
1 15oz. can of black beans, rinsed
1/2 tsp. cumin seeds
1 tbsp. fresh lemon juice
8 large eggs
8 yellow corn tortillas
sour cream, for serving
crumbled queso fresco, for serving
cilantro, for serving
1 clove garlic, finely chopped
kosher salt
pepper
4 cups baby spinach

Directions: Heat a small skillet over medium heat and add in 1 tablespoon of olive oil. Once the oil is hot, add in the cumin seeds and cook for 30 seconds, or until fragrant. Add in the black beans and cook for 5-7 minutes, or until heated through. Stir in the lemon juice and set the beans aside. In a separate large skillet, heat the remaining 1 tablespoon of olive oil over medium heat. Beat the eggs in a small mixing bowl and then add them to the skillet. Cook the eggs for 5-7 minutes, or until they are fully scrambled. Meanwhile, heat the tortillas in the microwave or on a griddle until they are warm and pliable. To assemble the tacos, place a spoonful of the scrambled eggs and a spoonful of the black bean mixture onto the center of each tortilla. Top the eggs and beans with a dollop of sour cream, a sprinkle of queso fresco, and a handful of baby spinach. Roll up the tortillas and serve them immediately. Enjoy with a side of salsa or guacamole for an extra burst of flavor.

Nutrition: 441 calories; fat 28g; saturated fat 11g; cholesterol 451mg; sodium 676mg; protein 20g; carbohydrates 30g; sugars 2g; fiber 7g; iron 3mg; calcium 218mg.

Zucchini Breakfast Salad

Preparation time: 10 minutes **Cooking time:** 0 minutes **Servings:** 4

Ingredients:
2 zucchinis, spiralized
1 cup beets, baked, peeled, and grated
1/2 bunch kale, chopped
2 tablespoons olive oil
For the tahini sauce:
1 tablespoon maple syrup
Juice of 1 lime
1/4-inch fresh ginger, grated
1/3 cup sesame seed paste

Directions: In a small mixing bowl, whisk together the maple syrup, lime juice, grated ginger, and sesame seed paste. Set the sauce aside. Next, heat a large skillet over medium heat and add in the olive oil. Once the oil is hot, add in the spiralized zucchinis and cook for 5-7 minutes, or until they are tender. Add in the chopped kale and cook for an additional 3-5 minutes, or until the kale is wilted. To assemble the salad, divide the cooked zucchini and kale between two bowls. Top each bowl with a scoop of the grated beets and then drizzle the tahini sauce over the top. Serve it up with a side of avocado or a sprinkle of nuts for an extra burst of flavor.

Nutrition: Calories 47.9; Total Fat 0.6 g; Saturated Fat 0.2 g; Polyunsaturated Fat 0.1g; Cholesterol 1.0 mg; Sodium 436.5 mg; Potassium 255.8 mg; Total Carbohydrate 9.7 g; Dietary Fiber 1.6 g; Sugars 2.2 g; Protein 1.5 g.

Breakfast Kale Frittata

Preparation time: 10 minutes **Cooking time:** 30 minutes **Servings:** 4

Ingredients:
6 kale stalks, chopped
1 small sweet onion, chopped
1 small broccoli head, florets separated
2 garlic cloves, minced
Salt and black pepper to taste
4 eggs
1 tablespoon olive oil

Directions: Heat a skillet over medium heat and add in the olive oil. Once the oil is hot, add in the chopped kale, onion, broccoli florets, and minced garlic. Cook the vegetables for 5-7 minutes, or until they are tender. Season the vegetables with salt and black pepper. In a mixing bowl, beat the eggs and then pour them over the vegetables in the skillet. Cook the frittata for 5-7 minutes, or until the eggs are fully set. Serve your Frittata with a side of toast or a sprinkle of cheese for an extra burst of flavor.

Nutrition: 293 calories; protein 17.9g; carbohydrates 7.9g; dietary fiber 2.3g; sugars 2.7g; fat 21.1g; saturated fat 7.1g; cholesterol 383.2mg; sodium 517mg.

Breakfast Corn Salad

Preparation time: 10 minutes **Cooking time:** 0 minutes **Servings:** 4

Ingredients:
2 avocados, pitted, peeled, and cubed
1 pint mixed cherry tomatoes, halved
2 cups fresh corn kernels
1 red onion, chopped
For the salad dressing:
2 tablespoons olive oil
1 tablespoon lime juice
1/2 teaspoon grated lime zest
A pinch of salt and black pepper
1/4 cup chopped cilantro

Directions: In a bowl, whisk together the olive oil, lime juice, lime zest, salt, and black pepper. Set the dressing aside. In another bowl, combine the cubed avocados, cherry tomatoes, corn kernels, and red onion. Pour the salad dressing over the top and toss the ingredients to fully coat them.

Nutrition per serving: Calories: 173, Total Fat: 14 g, Saturated Fat: 2 g, Cholesterol: 0 mg, Sodium: 76 mg, Total Carbohydrates: 16 g, Fiber: 6 g, Sugar: 3 g, Protein: 3 g

Carrots Breakfast Mix

Preparation time: 10 minutes **Cooking time:** 0 minutes **Servings:** 4

Ingredients:
1 1/2 tablespoons maple syrup
1 teaspoon olive oil

1 tablespoon chopped walnuts
1 onion, chopped
4 cups shredded carrots
1 tablespoon curry powder
1/4 teaspoon ground turmeric
Black pepper to taste
2 tablespoons sesame seed paste
1/4 cup lemon juice
1/2 cup chopped parsley

Directions: Heat a large skillet over medium heat and add in the olive oil. Once the oil is hot, add in the chopped onion and cook for 5-7 minutes, or until it is softened. Add in the shredded carrots and cook for an additional 5-7 minutes, or until the carrots are tender. Stir in the curry powder, turmeric, and black pepper and cook the mixture for 1-2 minutes, or until the spices are fragrant. Add in the maple syrup and sesame seed paste and cook the mixture for an additional 2-3 minutes, or until the carrots are fully coated in the sauce. To finish the dish, stir in the lemon juice and chopped parsley.

Nutrition: Calories: 160, Protein: 3g, Fat: 12g, Carbohydrates: 16g, Fiber: 4g, Sugar: 10g, Sodium: 150mg

Shakshuka

Total Time 1 hour **Difficulty Level** low **Servings** 8

Ingredients:
1 large onion
2 tablespoons olive oil
2 red bell peppers
2 tomatoes (28oz.)
3 cloves minced garlic
1 can diced tomatoes (14.5oz.)
1 tablespoon paprika
2 tablespoons cumin
1/2 tablespoon coriander
Kosher salt, to taste
1/2 tablespoon red pepper flakes
Sliced bread for serving
Black pepper, to taste
1/2 cup crumbled feta
8 large eggs
Chopped parsley, to taste

Directions: Heat the olive oil in a large skillet over medium heat. Add the onion and bell peppers and cook until they are tender, about 5 minutes. Add the garlic, paprika, cumin, coriander, and red pepper flakes to the skillet and cook for an additional 2 minutes, until the spices are fragrant. Stir in the diced tomatoes and the can of diced tomatoes. Bring the mixture to a boil, then reduce the heat to low and simmer for 10 minutes. Crack the eggs into the skillet, spacing them evenly apart. Sprinkle the feta cheese over the top. Cover the skillet and cook for 8-10 minutes, or until the eggs are set. Serve the shakshuka hot, garnished with chopped parsley and served with sliced bread.

Nutrition per serving: Calories: 222, Fat: 16.4g, Saturated fat: 4.9g, Cholesterol: 213mg, Sodium: 612mg, Carbohydrates: 12.3g, Fiber: 3.1g, Sugar: 6.3g, Protein: 11.6g

Fresh Fruits Mooring Salad with Oats

Total Time 20 minutes **Difficulty Level** low **Servings** 4

Ingredients:
1 cup berries (such as blueberries, raspberries, or blackberries)
1 cup steelcut oats
1/2 cup oranges, chopped
1 avocado, diced
1 banana, sliced
3 tablespoons olive oil
1 teaspoon lemon zest
1 handful fresh parsley, chopped
1/2 cup maple syrup

Directions: Cook the steelcut oats according to the package instructions. Once the oats are cooked, set them aside to cool. In a large mixing bowl, combine the cooked oats, chopped oranges, diced avocado, sliced banana, and berries. Drizzle the olive oil over the top and toss the ingredients to fully coat them. To finish the dish, sprinkle the lemon zest and chopped parsley over the top of the fruit salad. Serve the Fresh Fruits Morning Salad with a side of maple syrup for drizzling. Enjoy your Fresh Fruits Morning Salad with a sprinkle of nuts or seeds for an extra burst of flavor.

Nutrition per serving: Calories: 330, Fat: 16g, Saturated fat: 2g, Cholesterol: 0mg, Sodium: 10mg, Carbohydrates: 46g, Fiber: 8g, Sugar: 22g, Protein: 5g

Breakfast Cauliflower Rice Bowl

Preparation Time: 10 minutes **Cooking Time:** 12 minutes **Servings:** 6

Ingredients:
1 cup cauliflower rice
1/2 tsp red pepper flakes
1 1/2 tsp curry powder
1/2 tbsp grated ginger
1 cup vegetable stock
4 tomatoes, chopped
3 cups broccoli, chopped
Pepper
Salt

Directions: Heat a large skillet over medium heat and add in the red pepper flakes and curry powder. Cook the spices for 1-2 minutes, or until they are fragrant. Stir in the grated ginger, vegetable stock, and cauliflower rice. Bring the mixture to a boil and then reduce the heat to a simmer. Cook the cauliflower rice for 5-7 minutes, or until it is tender. Stir in the chopped tomatoes and broccoli and cook the mixture for an additional 5-7 minutes, or until the vegetables are tender. Season the Breakfast Cauliflower Rice Bowl with pepper and salt to taste.

Nutrition per serving: Calories: 67, Total Fat: 2g, Saturated Fat: 0g, Cholesterol: 0mg, Sodium: 217mg, Carbohydrates: 12g, Dietary Fiber: 3g, Sugars: 4g, Protein: 4g

APPETIZERS

Roasted Green Beans with Sesame seeds

Ready in about 25 minutes **Servings** 3

Ingredients
1 ½ pounds green beans, trimmed
2 tablespoons olive oil, or as needed

1/2 teaspoon garlic powder
Sea salt, to taste
1 1/2 tablespoon sesame seeds
1/2 teaspoon cayenne pepper

Directions: Preheat your oven to 400°F and line a baking sheet with parchment paper. In a small mixing bowl, combine the olive oil, garlic powder, and sea salt. Add the green beans to the bowl and toss them to fully coat them in the seasoning mixture. Spread the green beans out on the prepared baking sheet and sprinkle the sesame seeds and cayenne pepper over the top. Roast the green beans for 15-20 minutes, or until they are tender and crispy. Serve the Roasted Green Beans with Sesame Seeds immediately as a delicious and healthy side dish.

Nutrition: Calories 181; Fat 11.4g; Carbs 17.3g; Protein 6.1g; Sugars 7.4g

Mediterranean Summer Tomatoes

Total Time 15 minutes **Difficulty Level** low **Servings** 6

Ingredients:
1/2 cup of olive oil extra-virgin
5 coarsely chopped shallots
5 medium-sized whole fresh tomatoes
1/4 cup of balsamic vinegar
1 loaf of French bread for dipping

Instructions: Preheat your grill to medium heat. In a bowl, mix together the olive oil and shallots. Slice the tomatoes in half and brush them with the olive oil and shallot mixture. Place the tomatoes on the grill, cut-side down, and grill for 3-4 minutes. Flip the tomatoes over and grill for an additional 3-4 minutes, or until they are tender and have grill marks. Remove the tomatoes from the grill and drizzle with balsamic vinegar. Serve the grilled tomatoes with a loaf of French bread for dipping.

Nutrition per serving: Calories: 234, Fat: 15g, Carbohydrates: 24g, Protein: 4g, Fiber: 2g, Sugar: 8g, Sodium: 263mg

Spinach-Walnut Greek Yogurt Dip

Total Time 10 minutes **Difficulty Level** low **Servings** one large bowl

Ingredients:
2 cups of Greek yogurt
1/2 cup of parsley, chopped
1 clove of minced garlic
2 cups of baby spinach
Kosher salt
Pinch of black pepper
Extra virgin olive oil
1 teaspoon of dry mint
3/4 cup of finely chopped walnuts
1 tablespoon of lemon juice, freshly squeezed
For serving:
Homemade pita chips
Veggies

Instructions: Combine the Greek yogurt, parsley, minced garlic, baby spinach, salt, pepper, olive oil, and dry mint in a blender or food processor. Blend the mixture until it is smooth and creamy. Stir in the finely chopped walnuts and lemon juice. Adjust the seasoning to taste, adding more salt or pepper if desired. To serve, transfer the Spinach-Walnut Greek Yogurt Dip to a serving bowl and serve with homemade pita chips and veggies for dipping. Enjoy your Spinach-Walnut Greek Yogurt Dip with a sprinkle of herbs or cheese for an extra burst of flavor.

Nutrition per serving (assuming 6 servings): Calories: 170, Total fat: 11g, Saturated fat: 1.5g, Cholesterol: 5mg, Sodium: 75mg, Carbohydrates: 13g, Dietary fiber: 2g, Sugar: 6g, Protein: 8g

Wine Roasted Veggies

Ready in about 20 minutes **Servings** 5

Ingredients
1/4 cup olive oil
1/4 cup dry white wine
1 1/2 tablespoons balsamic vinegar
1/4 teaspoon dried oregano
1/2 teaspoon basil
1 teaspoon chives
Sea salt and cayenne pepper, to taste
2 red bell peppers, sliced
2 medium eggplants, diced
1 large red onion, sliced
3 sweet potatoes, peeled and sliced into chunks

Directions: Preheat your oven to 425°F and line a baking sheet with parchment paper. In a mixing bowl, combine the olive oil, white wine, balsamic vinegar, dried oregano, basil, chives, sea salt, and cayenne pepper. Add the sliced bell peppers, diced eggplants, sliced red onion, and sweet potatoes to the bowl and toss them to fully coat them in the seasoning mixture. Spread the veggies out on the prepared baking sheet and roast them for 20-25 minutes, or until they are tender and caramelized.

Nutrition: Calories 401; Fat 13.3g; Carbs 82.2g; Protein 11.5g; Sugars 13.1g

Herb And Feta Dip

Total Time 25 minutes **Difficulty Level** low **Servings:** 8

Ingredients:
1/2 cup of feta cheese, crumbled
1/4 cup of fresh mint, chopped
1 teaspoon of freshly ground pepper
1 15-ounce can of rinsed white beans
3/4 cup of plain yogurt, nonfat
1/4 cup of fresh dill, chopped
1 tablespoon of lemon juice
1 teaspoon of garlic salt
1/4 cup of fresh chives, chopped
1/4 cup of fresh parsley, chopped

Directions: Combine the feta cheese, mint, pepper, white beans, yogurt, dill, lemon juice, garlic salt, chives, and parsley in a blender or food processor. Blend the mixture until it is smooth and creamy. Adjust the seasoning to taste, adding more lemon juice, garlic salt, or pepper if desired. Serve the Herb and Feta Dip with veggies, crackers, or pita chips for dipping.

Nutrition: Calories: 60, Fat: 2g, Saturated fat: 1g, Cholesterol: 5mg, Sodium: 215mg, Carbohydrates: 7g, Fiber: 2g, Sugar: 2g, Protein: 4g

Patatokeftedes

Prep Time: 5 minutes **Cooking Time:** 15 minutes **Total Time:** 20 minutes **Servings:** 6

Ingredients:
1 lb. potatoes, shredded
1 red onion, thinly diced
2 tomatoes, thinly diced
1 cup wholegrain flour
Oil, as needed
3/4 cup water
Salt and pepper
1 tsp. oregano
Parsley

Directions: Combine the shredded potatoes, diced red onion, diced tomatoes, wholegrain flour, salt, pepper, and oregano in a large mixing bowl. Slowly stir in the water, a little at a time, until the mixture is fully combined and forms a thick dough. Heat a large skillet over medium heat and add in enough oil to cover the bottom of the pan. Using your hands, form the dough into small balls and place them in the hot skillet. Cook the Patatokeftedes for 5-7 minutes on each side, or until they are golden brown and crispy. Sprinkle the Patatokeftedes with parsley and serve them hot.

Nutrition per serving: Calories: 150, Total Fat: 6g, Saturated Fat: 1g, Cholesterol: 0mg, Sodium: 150mg, Carbohydrates: 22g, Dietary Fiber: 2g, Sugar: 1g, Protein: 3g

Stuffed Zucchini Boats

Total Time 20 minutes **Difficulty Level** low **Servings** 6

Ingredients:
1/4 medium chopped onion
1/8 cup of feta cheese, crumbled
2 tablespoons of pine nuts
1 teaspoon of dried basil
1/8 cup of diced green olives
6 medium-sized zucchini
1 teaspoon of dried oregano
1/2 cup of grated Asiago cheese, divided
2 chopped cloves of garlic

Directions: Preheat your oven to 375°F. Slice the zucchini in half lengthwise and scoop out the flesh, leaving about a 1/4-inch border. Finely chop the scooped out zucchini flesh and set it aside. Heat a skillet over medium heat and add in the onion. Cook the onion until it is translucent, about 5 minutes. Add in the chopped zucchini flesh, garlic, pine nuts, olives, basil, and oregano. Cook the mixture for an additional 5 minutes, or until the vegetables are tender. Stir in the feta cheese and 1/4 cup of the Asiago cheese. Fill the zucchini boats with the vegetable mixture and top them with the remaining Asiago cheese. Bake the Stuffed Zucchini Boats for 15-20 minutes, or until they are tender and the cheese is melted and golden brown. Enjoy your Stuffed Zucchini Boats with a sprinkle of herbs or cheese for an extra burst of flavor.

Nutrition per serving: Calories: 150, Total Fat: 10g, Saturated Fat: 3g, Cholesterol: 20mg, Sodium: 280mg, Total Carbohydrates: 12g, Dietary Fiber: 2g, Sugars: 5g, Protein: 7g

Beetroot, rocket, and blue cheese bites

Preparation Time: 10 minutes **Cooking Time:** 15 minutes **Servings:** 1

Ingredients:
2 ready-to-eat baby beetroot, quartered
16 baby rocket leaves
150g blue cheese, cut into small wedges

Directions: Preheat your oven to 350°F. Arrange the beetroot quarters on a baking sheet and bake them for about 15-20 minutes, or until they are tender. To assemble the bites, place a piece of beetroot on top of a baby rocket leaf and top it with a small wedge of blue cheese.

Nutrition: calories 1166, fat 96g, carbohydrate 18 g, protein 52.5g, fiber 4g

Smoked salmon and potato bites

Preparation Time: 10 minutes **Cooking Time:** 15 minutes **Servings:** 1

Ingredients:
4 small chat potatoes, steamed, quartered, cooled
1/4 small iceberg lettuce, cut into 2cm pieces
4 slices smoked salmon, halved
Fresh dill sprigs, to serve

Directions: Steam the potatoes until they are tender. Once they are cooked, allow them to cool and then quarter them. To assemble the bites, place a piece of iceberg lettuce on top of a quartered potato and top it with a half slice of smoked salmon. Garnish with fresh dill sprigs.

Nutrition: Calories: 300, Protein: 20g, Fat: 15g, Carbohydrates: 30g, Fiber: 4g, Sodium: 500mg

Greek Courgettes Balls

Prep time: 10 minutes **Cooking time:** 25 minutes **Total time:** 35 minutes **Servings:** 4

Ingredients:
2 cups zucchinis, shredded
1/2 cup shredded cheese
4 oz. Feta cheese, crumbled
3 spring onions, minced
2 garlic cloves, pressed
1 egg
1/2 cup flour
1/2 cup dry breadcrumbs
Oil, as needed
2 tsp. mint, chopped
2 tsp. parsley, chopped
1 tsp. dill, chopped
Salt to taste

Directions: Preheat your oven to 350°F. In a large bowl, mix together the zucchinis, shredded cheese, Feta cheese, spring onions, garlic, egg, flour, and breadcrumbs until well combined. Roll the mixture into small balls and place them on a baking sheet lined with parchment paper. Bake for 15-20 minutes, or until they are golden brown and crispy. Serve with yogurt and garlic sauce.

Nutrition per 1 courgette ball: Calories: 120, Fat: 7g, Carbohydrates: 11g, Protein: 5g, Sodium: 280mg

Mediterranean Nachos

Total Time 10 minutes **Difficulty Level** low **Servings** 4-6

Ingredients:
½ bag of tortilla chips
½ of 14.5 ounces can (~3/4 cup) of garbanzo beans, rinsed, drained and patted dry
½ of a 10-ounce container of Sabra Hummus
1 cup canned artichoke hearts, drained
½ cup crumbled feta cheese
½ cup chopped roasted red peppers
2½ Tablespoons pine nuts
2 tablespoons fresh minced cilantro
½ cup chopped tomatoes

Directions: Preheat your oven to 350°F. Arrange the tortilla chips in a single layer on a large baking sheet. In a bowl, mix together the garbanzo beans, hummus, and artichoke hearts until well combined. Spread the bean mixture over the tortilla chips and top with the feta cheese, roasted red peppers, pine nuts, and cilantro. Bake the Mediterranean Nachos for 10-15 minutes, or until the cheese is melted and the chips are crispy. To serve, top the Mediterranean Nachos with the chopped tomatoes.

Nutrition per serving, based on 6 servings: Calories: 348, Fat: 17.6g, Saturated Fat: 4.3g, Cholesterol: 25mg, Sodium: 859mg, Carbohydrates: 36.2g, Fiber: 8.3g, Sugar: 3.4g, Protein: 12.2g

Za'atar flatbreads

Prep time: 5 minutes **Cook time:** 12 minutes **Serves** 6

Ingredients:
1 (16-ounce / 454g) bag of whole-wheat pizza dough
3 tablespoons olive oil
3 tablespoons sesame seeds
3 tablespoons dried thyme
1/4 teaspoon kosher or sea salt
Nonstick cooking spray

Directions: Preheat your oven to 450°F. Spray a large baking sheet with nonstick cooking spray. In a small bowl, mix together the sesame seeds, thyme, and salt. On a lightly floured surface, roll out the pizza dough into a large rectangle. Brush the dough with olive oil and sprinkle the sesame seed mixture evenly over the top. Use a pizza cutter or sharp knife to cut the dough into small squares or triangles. Arrange the flatbreads on the prepared baking sheet and bake for 8-10 minutes, or until they are crispy and golden brown. **TIP:** To save time, you can use wholewheat pita bread or lavash bread and a packaged za'atar spice blend.

Nutrition: Calories: 231, Total Fat: 9.6g, Saturated Fat: 1.4g, Cholesterol: 0mg, Sodium: 307mg, Total Carbohydrates: 29.3g, Dietary Fiber: 3.2g, Sugars: 1.6g, Protein: 8.2g

Dukkah-swirled labne dip

Preparation Time: 10 minutes **Cooking Time:** 15 minutes **Servings:** 1

Ingredients:
500g plain Greek-style yogurt
1 tsp sea salt
2 tbsp almond, lemon, and herb dukkah
1 tbsp extra virgin olive oil
Lemon zest, to serve

Directions: Combine the yogurt and salt in a small bowl. In a separate bowl, mix together the dukkah and olive oil. Spread the yogurt mixture in a shallow dish, then drizzle the dukkah mixture over the top. Use a skewer or chopstick to swirl the dukkah mixture into the yogurt. Sprinkle with lemon zest and serve chilled with crackers, pita chips, or fresh veggies for dipping.

Nutrition per serving: Calories: 250, Total fat: 14g, Saturated fat: 5g, Cholesterol: 35mg, Sodium: 940mg, Total carbohydrate: 16g, Dietary fiber: 3g, Sugar: 12g, Protein: 19g

Quick antipasto pasta

Preparation Time: 10 minutes **Cooking Time:** 15 minutes **Servings:** 4

Ingredients:
300g farfalle pasta
1/3 cup basil leaves
1/4 cup (40g) pine nuts, toasted
1/4 cup (20g) finely grated parmesan
1 garlic clove, crushed
120g pkt Coles Australian Baby Rocket
1/2 cup (125ml) olive oil
100g thickly sliced Don Ham on the Bone from the Deli, torn
50g slices Coles Deli Herb Coated Salami, chopped
100g Coles Danish Fetta, coarsely crumbled
140g Coles Deli Giant Pitted Kalamata Olives, halved
170g Coles Deli Semi Dried Tomatoes with Fresh Basil, coarsely chopped

Directions: Bring a large pot of salted water to a boil and cook the pasta according to the package instructions. Drain and set aside. In a blender or food processor, combine the basil, pine nuts, parmesan, and garlic. Pulse until the mixture becomes a smooth paste. In a large bowl, toss together the pasta, rocket, and basil paste. Heat the olive oil in a large skillet over medium heat. Add the ham, salami, and fetta and cook until the ham is browned and the fetta is melted, about 5 minutes. Stir in the olives and semi-dried tomatoes, then pour the mixture over the pasta and toss to combine.

Nutrition: Calories: 687, Fat: 48.3g, Saturated fat: 12.2g, Cholesterol: 61mg, Sodium: 1286mg, Carbohydrates: 51.3g, Fiber: 5.8g, Sugar: 5.4g, Protein: 19.8g

Avocado and Tuna Tapas

Preparation Time: 11 minutes **Cooking Time**: 20 minutes **Servings:** 1

Ingredients:
1 (12 ounces) can solid white tuna packed in water drained
3 green onions, thinly sliced
1 tablespoon mayonnaise (additional for garnish)
½ red bell pepper, chopped
2 ripe avocados, halved and pitted
black pepper to taste
1 dash balsamic vinegar
1 pinch garlic salt, or to taste

Directions: Mix together the drained tuna, green onions, mayonnaise, and red bell pepper in a small bowl. Set aside. Next, scoop out the avocado flesh into a separate bowl and mash it until it reaches your desired consistency. Add a pinch of black pepper and a dash of balsamic vinegar to the mashed avocado and mix well. To assemble the tapas, spread a generous amount of the mashed avocado onto a slice of your favorite bread. Top with a spoonful of the tuna mixture and a sprinkle of garlic salt. Garnish with additional green onions, if desired. Repeat this process until you have used up all of the ingredients. Serve the avocado and tuna tapas immediately, or cover and refrigerate until ready to serve. These tapas are best served cold and make a delicious appetizer or snack for any occasion.

Nutrition: Calories: 332, Total Fat: 26g, Saturated Fat: 4g, Cholesterol: 40mg, Sodium: 450mg, Carbohydrates: 20g, Fiber: 10g, Sugars: 5g, Protein: 16g

Zucchini-Feta Rolls

Preparation Time: 10 minutes **Cooking Time:** 18 minutes **Servings:** 1

Ingredients:
olive oil, divided
1 (4 ounces) package crumbled feta cheese
5 zucchinis, thinly sliced lengthwise 3 cloves garlic, minced
4 tablespoons balsamic vinegar
2 tablespoons dried Italian herbs

Directions: Heat a large skillet over medium heat and add a drizzle of olive oil. While the skillet warms up, mix together the feta cheese, minced garlic, and Italian herbs in a small bowl. Once the skillet is hot, place a zucchini slice in the pan and top it with a spoonful of the feta mixture. Roll the zucchini slice tightly and secure it with a toothpick. Repeat this process with the remaining zucchini slices and feta mixture. Cook the rolls for 3-4 minutes on each side, or until they are golden brown. Once they are finished cooking, drizzle the rolls with balsamic vinegar and serve immediately. Marinate in the refrigerator for 1 to 2 days, covered.

Nutrition: Calories: 303, Total Fat: 23g, Saturated Fat: 13g, Cholesterol: 73mg, Sodium: 556mg, Carbohydrates: 18g, Fiber: 4g, Sugars: 12g, Protein: 12g

Warm lamb, pesto, and antipasto salad

Preparation Time: 10 minutes **Cooking Time:** 15 minutes **Servings:** 1

Ingredients:
2 x 280g jars Coles mixed chargrilled vegetables
275g jar Coles marinated artichoke hearts
1 tbsp lemon juice
2 tbsp Wattle Valley chunky basil with cashew & parmesan dip
1 tbsp olive oil
500g packet Coles grill lamb souvlaki strips
120g baby spinach leaves
400g Coles butter beans, drained, rinsed

Directions: Heat a large skillet over medium heat. Add 1 tablespoon of olive oil to the skillet and then add the chargrilled vegetables and artichoke hearts. Cook for 2-3 minutes, stirring occasionally, until the vegetables are heated through. In a small bowl, mix together the lemon juice and chunky basil with cashew & parmesan dip. Set aside. Next, add the lamb souvlaki strips to the skillet and cook for 2-3 minutes, or until the lamb is cooked to your desired level of doneness. To assemble the salad, place the baby spinach leaves in a large bowl. Add the cooked vegetables, lamb, and butter beans to the bowl. Drizzle the pesto mixture over the top of the salad and toss everything together.

Nutrition: Calories: 1259, Total Fat: 66g, Saturated Fat: 19g, Cholesterol: 115mg, Sodium: 3041mg, Total Carbohydrates: 87g, Dietary Fiber: 27g, Sugars: 18g, Protein: 71g

Gorgonzola Dip

Total Time 15 minutes **Difficulty Level** low **Servings** 20

Ingredients:
1 cup of sour cream lowfat
4 ounces of crumbled Gorgonzola cheese

One peeled clove of garlic
Salt and pepper to taste
One tablespoon of fresh dill chopped
1 cup of mayonnaise lowfat
Two teaspoons of unflavored gelatin

Directions: Start by combining the sour cream, Gorgonzola cheese, and garlic in a blender or food processor. Blend until smooth and well combined. Season with salt and pepper to taste, then add in the fresh dill and pulse a few times to incorporate. Next, transfer the mixture to a small saucepan and heat over medium heat. Add in the mayonnaise and gelatin, stirring until well combined. Bring the mixture to a simmer, then reduce the heat to low and let it cook for about 5 minutes, or until the gelatin is fully dissolved and the dip is smooth and creamy. Serve the Gorgonzola dip warm or chilled, alongside your favorite dipping items like crudités, crackers, or bread. You can also try topping it with some additional crumbled Gorgonzola or a sprinkle of fresh dill for added flavor.

Nutrition per serving, approximately 2 tablespoons: Calories: 119, Fat: 11g, Saturated Fat: 4g, Cholesterol: 25mg, Sodium: 205mg, Carbohydrates: 3g, Fiber: 0g, Sugar: 1g, Protein: 3g

Herb marinated fetta

Preparation Time: 10 minutes **Cooking Time:** 15 minutes **Servings:** 1
Ingredients:
350g feta
1/3 cup olive oil
1 1/2 tbsp lemon juice
2 tsp thyme leaves
1 tsp rosemary, chopped
cracked black pepper
2 tbsp green olives, finely chopped
baked bagel chips or croutons, to serve

Directions: Start by cutting the feta into small bite-sized cubes. In a small mixing bowl, combine the olive oil, lemon juice, thyme, rosemary, and black pepper. Mix well to create the marinade. Place the feta cubes in a shallow dish and pour the marinade over top. Allow the feta to marinate for at least 30 minutes, or up to 4 hours in the refrigerator. After the feta has marinated, sprinkle the chopped olives over the top. Serve the feta with baked bagel chips or croutons as a tasty appetizer or snack.

Nutrition per serving: Calories: 81, Total Fat: 8g, Saturated Fat: 3g, Cholesterol: 19mg, Sodium: 128mg, Total Carbohydrates: 2g, Dietary Fiber: 0g, Sugars: 1g, Protein: 2g

Prosciutto and cranberry asparagus

Preparation Time: 10 minutes **Cooking Time:** 15 minutes **Servings:** 1
Ingredients:
2 tbsp jellied cranberry sauce
1 tsp chopped fresh thyme leaves
8 thin slices prosciutto
16 asparagus spears, trimmed
1 tbsp extra virgin olive oil

Directions: Start by preheating your oven to 400°F. Next, mix together the cranberry sauce and thyme in a small bowl. Spread a thin layer of the cranberry mixture onto each slice of prosciutto. Wrap a slice of prosciutto around each asparagus spear and place them onto a baking sheet lined with parchment paper. Drizzle the asparagus with olive oil and sprinkle with salt and pepper. Bake the asparagus for about 8-10 minutes, or until the prosciutto is crispy and the asparagus is tender.

Nutrition: Calories: 280, Total Fat: 17g, Saturated Fat: 5g, Cholesterol: 41mg, Sodium: 786mg, Total Carbohydrates: 24g, Dietary Fiber: 4g, Sugars: 18g, Protein: 10g

Crispy Ring Onions

Total Time: 30 minutes **Difficulty Level:** low **Servings:** 4

Ingredients:
2 cups of buttermilk, divided
2 large onions
One tablespoon of Olive Oil extra-virgin
1/2 teaspoon of each pepper, paprika, seasoning salt, and parsley 1/2 cup + 2 tablespoons of flour
2 cups of Panko bread crumbs
2 eggs

Directions: Slice the onions into 1/4 inch thick rings and set aside. In a large bowl, mix together 1 cup of buttermilk, olive oil, pepper, paprika, seasoning salt, and parsley. Dip the onion rings into the buttermilk mixture, making sure they are evenly coated. In a separate bowl, mix together the flour and Panko bread crumbs. Beat the eggs in a small bowl and add the remaining 1 cup of buttermilk. Dip the coated onion rings into the flour mixture, then into the egg mixture, and then back into the flour mixture. Place the coated onion rings on a baking sheet lined with parchment paper and bake for 15-20 minutes, or until golden brown and crispy. Serve with your favorite dipping sauce.

Nutrition per serving: Calories: 298, Total Fat: 9g, Saturated Fat: 2g, Cholesterol: 95mg, Sodium: 480mg, Total Carbohydrates: 44g, Dietary Fiber: 2g, Sugars: 6g, Protein: 10g

LUNCH

Chris' Kraut

Preparation Time: 10 minutes **Cooking Time**: 15 minutes **Servings**: 1

Ingredients:
½ pound bacon
1 (16 ounce) can sauerkraut, drained and rinsed
½ cup white sugar
salt and pepper to taste

Directions: Start by cooking the bacon in a skillet over medium heat until it is crispy. Once the bacon is cooked, remove it from the skillet and drain it on a paper towel. Set it aside for now. Next, add the sauerkraut to the skillet and cook it over medium heat until it is heated through. Once the sauerkraut is hot, add the white sugar and stir it in well. Season the sauerkraut with salt and pepper to taste. Break the bacon into small pieces and add it to the skillet with the sauerkraut. Stir everything together well and cook it for an additional 5 minutes or so, until the flavors are well combined and the sauerkraut is nice and hot. Serve alongside your favorite grilled meats or as a topping for bratwurst or hot dogs.

Nutrition: Calories: 427, Total Fat: 22g, Saturated Fat: 7g, Cholesterol: 45mg, Sodium: 1428mg, Total Carbohydrates: 46g, Dietary Fiber: 4g, Sugars: 42g, Protein: 11g

Tomato Zucchini Casserole

Preparation Time: 10 minutes **Cooking Time**: 15 minutes **Servings**: 1

Ingredients:

1½ cups grated Cheddar cheese
⅓ cup grated Parmesan cheese
½ teaspoon dried oregano
½ teaspoon dried basil
2 cloves of garlic, minced
Salt and pepper to taste
2 medium zucchinis, thinly sliced
5 plum tomatoes, thinly sliced
¼ cup butter
2 tablespoons of finely chopped onion
¾ cup fine bread crumbs

Directions: Preheat your oven to 350°F (180°C). Grease a 9x9 inch baking dish with cooking spray or butter. In a small bowl, mix together the Cheddar cheese, Parmesan cheese, oregano, basil, garlic, salt, and pepper. Arrange a layer of zucchini slices in the bottom of the prepared baking dish. Top with a layer of tomato slices, then sprinkle with half of the cheese mixture. Repeat the layering process, ending with a layer of cheese on top. In a small saucepan over medium heat, melt the butter. Add the onion and cook until it is translucent, about 5 minutes. Stir in the bread crumbs and cook for an additional 2-3 minutes, or until the crumbs are golden brown. Sprinkle the bread crumb mixture over the top of the casserole. Bake the casserole for 30-35 minutes, or until the cheese is melted and bubbly and the vegetables are tender. Serve hot, garnished with fresh herbs if desired.

Nutrition: Calories: 538, Total Fat: 35g, Saturated Fat: 21g, Cholesterol: 105mg, Sodium: 1048mg, Total Carbohydrates: 41g, Dietary Fiber: 4g, Sugars: 6g, Protein: 23g

Mediterranean Salad

Prep Time: 10 minutes **Cook time**: 0 minutes **Serving:** 4

Ingredients
Olive oil, 1/3 cup
Red wine vinegar, 2 tablespoons
Minced fresh garlic, 1/2 teaspoon
Italian seasoning, 1/2 teaspoon
Salt, a pinch
Black pepper, a pinch
Salad greens, 2 1/2 cups
Sliced black olives, 1 small can
Grape tomatoes, 1 cup
Sliced cucumbers, 1 cup
Red onions, 1/2 cup
Crumbled feta cheese, 1/4 cup

Directions: Start by whisking together the olive oil, red wine vinegar, minced garlic, Italian seasoning, salt, and black pepper in a small bowl. Set aside. In a large salad bowl, combine the salad greens, black olives, grape tomatoes, sliced cucumbers, and red onions. Pour the dressing over the top of the salad and toss to evenly coat. Sprinkle the crumbled feta cheese over the top of the salad. Add in any other desired toppings, such as grilled chicken or shrimp, to make it a complete meal.

Nutrition: Fat: 22g, Net Carbs: 7g, Protein: 2g, Sodium: 294mg

Baked Pangrattato Lamb

Prep Time: 10 minutes **Cook time**: 35 minutes **Serving**: 1

Ingredients

50g pitted kalamata olives
1 lemon
6 unpeeled garlic cloves
300g Charlotte potatoes
3 tablespoons olive oil
4 lamb cutlets
25g Sacla Garlic
25g Herb Pangrattato
Chopped parsley to garnish (optional)

Directions: Preheat your oven to 200ºC/400ºF. Thinly slice the potatoes and place them in a roasting tin. Toss with the olive oil, a pinch of salt, and a few grinds of black pepper. Roast the potatoes for 15 minutes, then remove the tin from the oven. While the potatoes are roasting, prepare the lamb. Place the cutlets in a shallow dish and squeeze the juice of half the lemon over them. Peel and chop the garlic, then scatter it over the lamb. When the potatoes have been in the oven for 15 minutes, place the lamb on top of the potatoes. In a small bowl, mix together the Sacla Garlic and Herb Pangrattato. Sprinkle this mixture over the lamb. Return the tin to the oven and roast for a further 15-20 minutes, or until the lamb is cooked to your liking and the potatoes are tender and golden. While the lamb is cooking, pit and chop the olives. When the lamb is cooked, remove the tin from the oven and scatter the olives over the top. Squeeze the juice of the remaining lemon half over the top, then sprinkle with chopped parsley (if using). Serve immediately, with any juices from the tin spooned over the top.

Nutrition: Fat: 24g, Net Carbs: 8g, Protein: 41g, Sodium: 698mg

Pasta with pine nuts and scallops

Ingredients:
8 ounces tagliatelle or fettuccine
4 tablespoons extravirgin vegetable oil
3 cloves new garlic, finely cleaved
1 leek, white part just, meagrely cut
10 pitted dark olives, divided
¼ cup pine nuts
12 enormous ocean scallops, split
Salt and newly ground pepper to taste
2 tablespoons slashed new basil

Directions: Bring a pot of salted water to a boil and cook the pasta according to package instructions. Drain and set aside. In a large frying pan, heat the oil over medium heat. Add the garlic and leek and cook until the leek is tender, about 5 minutes. Add half the olives and the pine nuts to the pan and cook for another 2 minutes. Place the scallops in the pan and cook until they are opaque and just cooked through, about 2-3 minutes per side. Season the scallop mixture with salt and pepper. Add the cooked pasta to the pan and toss to combine with the scallop mixture. Divide the pasta and scallop mixture among bowls and top with the remaining olives and the basil.

Nutrition: 409 calories for every serving 17g protein, 23g absolute fat, 3g soaked fat, 0 transfat, 41g starches, 45mg cholesterol, 139mg sodium, 1g fibre.

Lemony Shrimp and Risotto Bowl

Preparation time: 10 minutes **Cooking time:** 20 minutes **Servings:** 4

Ingredients:
2 c. rice

1 lemon, cut in wedges, to garnish
12 tiger shrimp, peeled and cooked
¼ c. olive oil
2 tomatoes, sliced
2 bell peppers, thinly sliced
½ c. black olives, pitted and halved
1 red onion, chopped
1 tsp dried dill
1 tbsp. fresh parsley, chopped
Salt and black pepper to taste

Directions: Cook the rice according to package instructions. In a frying pan, heat the olive oil over medium heat. Add the bell peppers, red onion, and tomatoes to the pan and cook until they are tender, about 5 minutes. Add the cooked shrimp to the pan and cook for an additional 2 minutes. Season the shrimp and vegetable mixture with the dill, parsley, salt, and black pepper. Divide the cooked rice among bowls, top with the shrimp and vegetable mixture and garnish with the lemon wedges.

Nutrition: Calories: 538, Total Fat: 27g, Saturated Fat: 4g, Cholesterol: 141mg, Sodium: 561mg, Total Carbohydrates: 51g, Dietary Fiber: 3g, Sugars: 6g, Protein: 22g

Salmon Pasta
Preparation Time: 10 minutes **Cooking Time:** 25 minutes **Servings:** 2

Ingredients:
5 tablespoons butter
¼ onion
1 tablespoon all purpose flour
1 teaspoon garlic powder
2 cups skim milk
¼ cup Romano cheese
1 cup green peas
¼ cup canned mushrooms
8 oz. salmon
1 package penne pasta

Directions: Cook the pasta according to package instructions. In a saucepan, melt the butter over medium heat. Add the onion and cook until it is translucent, about 5 minutes. Stir in the flour and garlic powder and cook for an additional minute. Gradually add the milk, stirring constantly, until the sauce thickens. Stir in the Romano cheese, green peas, and canned mushrooms. Cut the salmon into small pieces and add it to the sauce. Drain the pasta and add it to the sauce, stirring to combine. Serve the pasta and sauce immediately, garnished with additional Romano cheese if desired.

Nutrition: Calories: 211, Total Carbohydrate: 7 g, Cholesterol: 13 mg, Total Fat: 18 g, Fiber: 3 g, Protein: 17 g, Sodium: 289 mg

Melon Caprese Salad
Preparation time: 20 minutes **Cooking time:** 0 minutes **Serves:** 6

Ingredients:
1 cantaloupe, quartered and seeded
½ small seedless watermelon
1 cup grape tomatoes
2 cups fresh mozzarella balls (about 8 ounces / 227 g)

⅓ cup fresh basil or mint leaves, torn into small pieces
2 tbsp extravirgin olive oil
1 tbsp balsamic vinegar
¼ tsp freshly ground black pepper
¼ tsp kosher or sea salt

Directions: Cut the cantaloupe and watermelon into small pieces. In a large bowl, mix together the cantaloupe, watermelon, grape tomatoes, and mozzarella balls. Add the basil or mint leaves to the bowl. In a small bowl, whisk together the olive oil, balsamic vinegar, black pepper, and salt. Pour the dressing over the melon mixture and toss to combine. Serve the salad immediately, garnished with additional fresh basil or mint leaves if desired.

Nutrition: Calories: 297, fat: 12g, protein: 14g, carbs: 39g, fiber: 3g, sodium: 123mg

Shrimp Scampi and Pasta

Prep Time: 5 minutes **Cooking Time:** 10 minutes **Additional Time:** 0 minutes **Total Time:** 15 minutes **Servings:** 4

Ingredients:
14 oz. pasta
2 lb. shrimp, deveined
4 tbsp. of butter
45 garlic cloves, minced
2 tbsp. of olive oil
1/2 cup of dry white wine
1/2 tsp. smashed red pepper flakes
1 lemon, zested
2 lemons, juiced
1/2 thinly sliced lemon
Salt and pepper
1/4 cup parsley, chopped

Directions: Cook the pasta according to package instructions. In a large frying pan, melt the butter over medium heat. Add the garlic and cook until it is fragrant, about 1 minute. Add the olive oil, white wine, red pepper flakes, lemon zest, and lemon juice to the pan. Bring the mixture to a boil. Add the shrimp to the pan and cook until they are pink and cooked through, about 2-3 minutes per side. Season the shrimp with salt and pepper. Drain the pasta and add it to the pan with the shrimp. Toss to combine. Garnish the pasta and shrimp with the sliced lemon and parsley. Serve the pasta and shrimp immediately, with additional lemon wedges on the side if desired.

Nutrition: Calories: 788, Total Fat: 33g, Saturated Fat: 15g, Cholesterol: 456mg, Sodium: 1642mg, Total Carbohydrates: 84g, Dietary Fiber: 4g, Sugars: 6g, Protein: 37g

Seafood Paella

Preparation time: 5 minutes **Cooking time:** 35 minutes **Servings:** 4

Ingredients
2 c. whole wheat rice
4 oz. small shrimp, peeled and deveined
4 oz. bay scallops, tough muscle removed
¼ c. vegetable broth
1 c. freshly diced tomatoes and juice
Pinch of crumbled saffron threads
¼ tsp freshly ground pepper

¼ tsp salt
½ tsp fennel seed
½ tsp dried thyme
1 clove garlic, minced
1 medium onion, chopped
2 tsps. extravirgin olive oil

Directions: Cook the rice according to package instructions. In a saucepan, heat the olive oil over medium heat. Add the onion and garlic and cook until they are tender, about 5 minutes. Add the shrimp and scallops to the pan and cook until they are pink and cooked through, about 2-3 minutes per side. Stir in the vegetable broth, tomatoes, saffron, pepper, salt, fennel seed, and thyme. Bring the mixture to a boil. Reduce the heat to low and simmer the mixture for 5 minutes. Add the cooked rice to the pan and stir to combine. Serve the paella garnished with additional herbs if desired.

Nutrition per serving: Calories: 413, Total Fat: 10g, Saturated Fat: 2g, Cholesterol: 127mg, Sodium: 463mg, Total Carbohydrates: 62g, Dietary Fiber: 4g, Sugars: 5g, Protein: 23g

Pasta primavera with shrimp
Cooking time: 10 minutes **Servings:** 4

Ingredients:
1 pound whole wheat penne pasta
½ cup canned low sodium, fat free chicken broth
Extra virgin vegetable oil to drizzle + 2 teaspoons
2 dozen medium shrimp, cleaned, stripped, and deveined
1½ cups broccoli florets
1 medium red bell pepper, thinly sliced
1 cup diced catch mushrooms
1 cup frozen peas
½ cup sliced scallions
4 cloves garlic, minced
1 ounce (2 tablespoons) dry white wine
2 tablespoons freshly grated Parmesan cheese

Directions: Cook the pasta according to package instructions. In a large frying pan, heat a drizzle of olive oil over medium heat. Add the broccoli, bell pepper, mushrooms, and peas and cook until they are tender, about 5 minutes. Add the scallions and garlic to the pan and cook for an additional 2 minutes. Add the shrimp to the pan and cook until they are pink and cooked through, about 2-3 minutes per side. Stir in the chicken broth and white wine. Bring the mixture to a boil. Reduce the heat to low and simmer the mixture for 5 minutes. Add the cooked pasta to the pan and toss to combine with the shrimp and vegetable mixture. Serve the pasta garnished with the Parmesan cheese.

Nutrition: 526 calories for each serving, 24g protein, 8g all-out fat, 1g soaked fat, 0 transfat, 78g sugars, 34mg cholesterol, 218mg sodium, 12g fibre.

Mediterranean Fish with Tomatoes and Olives
Prep Time: 20 minutes **Cook time:** 40 minutes **Serving:** 2

Ingredients:
9 Tomatoes
1 teaspoon Caster sugar
1 cup Olive oil
700g Kipfler potatoes

2 slices of Woodfired bread
3 Garlic cloves
1/2 cup Parsley
10Basil leaves
1 Whole fish
20 Whole black olives
1 cup dry white wine
1 Lemon

Directions: Preheat your oven to 200ºC/400ºF. Cut the tomatoes into wedges and place them in a baking dish. Sprinkle with the sugar. Roast the tomatoes in the oven for 20-25 minutes, or until they are tender and caramelized. Meanwhile, heat the olive oil in a frying pan over medium heat. Add the potatoes and cook until they are tender and browned, about 10-15 minutes. Toast the bread in the oven for 5-10 minutes, or until it is crispy. In a food processor, blend together the garlic, parsley, basil, and a few tablespoons of olive oil until it forms a paste. Rub the paste all over the fish. Place the fish in a baking dish. Scatter the olives around the fish. Pour the white wine over the top. Roast the fish in the oven for 20-25 minutes, or until it is cooked through. Place the fish on a serving platter and surround it with the roasted tomatoes, potatoes, and toasted bread with squeezed lemon over the top.

Nutrition: Calories: 1052, Fat: 66g, Saturated Fat: 10g, Cholesterol: 105mg, Sodium: 667mg, Carbohydrates: 87g, Fiber: 14g, Sugar: 18g, Protein: 35g

Pesto Pasta

Preparation time: 10 minutes **Cooking time:** 8 minutes **Servings:** 4 to 6

Ingredients:
1 pound (454 g) spaghetti
4 cups fresh basil leaves, stems removed
3 cloves garlic
1 teaspoon salt
½ teaspoon freshly ground black pepper
½ cup toasted pine nuts
¼ cup lemon juice
½ cup grated Parmesan cheese
1 cup extra virgin olive oil

Direction: Cook the spaghetti according to package instructions. In a food processor, combine the basil, garlic, salt, pepper, pine nuts, and lemon juice. Pulse until the mixture is well combined. With the blender or food processor running, slowly drizzle in the olive oil. Stir in the Parmesan cheese. Drain the spaghetti and return it to the pot. Add the pesto sauce and toss to combine. Serve the pasta immediately, garnished with additional Parmesan cheese and toasted pine nuts if desired.

Nutrition: Calories: 1067, fat: 72.0g, protein: 23.0g, carbs: 91.0g, fiber: 6.0g, sodium: 817mg

Sicilian style linguine with eggplant and roasted peppers

Ingredients:
2 huge yellow chime peppers
1 little eggplant, stripped and dig ½inch blocks
2 tablespoons extra virgin vegetable oil
2 tablespoons minced new oregano
2 tablespoons escapades
4 teaspoons minced new garlic

1 (35ounce) can strip plum tomatoes
½ teaspoon squashed scorching pepper chips
Salt and newly ground pepper to taste
1 pound linguine
1 cup destroyed new basil leaves
¾ cup ground Romano cheddar

Directions: Preheat your grill or broiler. Grill or broil the bell peppers and eggplant until they are tender and browned, about 5-10 minutes per side. In a large saucepan, heat the olive oil over medium heat. Add the oregano, capers, and garlic and cook until they are fragrant, about 1 minute. Add the grilled peppers and eggplant to the pan. Pour in the tomatoes and add the red pepper flakes, salt, and pepper. Bring the mixture to a boil. Reduce the heat to low and simmer the mixture for 5 minutes. Meanwhile, cook the linguine according to package instructions. Add the cooked linguine to the saucepan with the vegetables and toss to combine. Serve the linguine

Nutrition: 336 calories for each serving, 13g protein, 10g all-out fat, 3g soaked fat, 0 trans-fat, 50g sugars, 15mg cholesterol, 461mg sodium, 6g fiber.

Slow Cooker Mediterranean Pasta

Preparation Time: 10 minutes **Cooking Time:** 4 hours **Servings:** 8

Ingredients:
1 pound of pasta
2 minced garlic cloves
1 chopped onion
Salt as per taste
Pepper as per taste
1¼ pounds Chicken tenders
25 ounces of Marinara sauce
1 teaspoon of Italian seasoning
12 ounces of Cream cheese
2 Bay leaves
¼ teaspoon Pepper
¼ teaspoon Salt

Directions: In a slow cooker, combine the pasta, garlic, onion, salt, pepper, chicken, marinara sauce, Italian seasoning, cream cheese, bay leaves, pepper, and salt. Stir to combine. Cover the slow cooker and cook on low heat for 6-8 hours, or until the chicken is cooked through and the pasta is tender. Stir the pasta before serving. Serve the pasta garnished with additional herbs and grated cheese if desired.

Nutrition: Calories: 465, Carbohydrate: 50g, Protein: 26g, Sugars: 7g, Fat: 17g, Dietary Fiber: 3g, Cholesterol: 92mg, Sodium: 687mg, Potassium: 760mg

Robust Mediterranean Sausage & Pasta

Preparation Time: 15 minutes **Cooking Time:** 6½ hours **Servings:** 4

Ingredients:
4 ounces Italian sausage links, cut into half
10 ounces undrained tomatoes and chilies, chopped
25.6 ounces Italian sausage spaghetti sauce
1 medium onion, chopped
1 large green pepper, julienned
1 teaspoon Italian seasoning
2 cups spiral pasta, uncooked

2 minced cloves of garlic

Directions: In a skillet, cook the sausage over medium heat until browned on all sides. Remove the sausage from the skillet and set aside. In the same skillet, add the onion and green pepper and cook until the vegetables are tender. Add the minced garlic and cook for an additional minute. Stir in the chopped tomatoes and chilies, Italian sausage spaghetti sauce, and Italian seasoning. Bring the sauce to a simmer and add the sausage back into the skillet. Cook the pasta according to package instructions, then drain and add it to the skillet with the sausage and sauce. Toss the pasta with the sauce until it is coated. Serve the pasta and sausage garnished with fresh herbs or parmesan cheese.

Nutrition: Calories: 529, Carbohydrates: 60g, Protein: 23g, Sugars: 19g, Fat: 22g, Cholesterol: 53g, Sodium: 1573mg

Mediterranean Tagliatelle

Prep Time: 10 minutes **Cook time:** 15 minutes **Serving:** 4

Ingredients:
250g dried tagliatelle pasta
55g pine nuts
1 tablespoon olive oil
1 red onion, diced
1 garlic clove, minced
280g marinated artichoke pieces
95g Kalamata olives, pitted and halved
80g sundried tomatoes, sliced
1 tablespoon drained chopped capers
250g feta cheese, crumbled
1 bunch basil, roughly chopped
Salt and black pepper, to taste

Directions: Bring a large pot of salted water to a boil and cook the tagliatelle according to package instructions. Drain and set aside. In a large skillet, heat the olive oil over medium heat. Add the red onion and cook until it is soft and translucent. Stir in the minced garlic and cook for an additional minute. Add the artichoke pieces, Kalamata olives, sundried tomatoes, and capers to the skillet and cook until the vegetables are tender. Stir in the cooked tagliatelle, pine nuts, and crumbled feta cheese. Gently toss the pasta with the vegetables and cheese until everything is well combined. Season the tagliatelle with salt and black pepper, to taste. Serve the tagliatelle garnished with fresh basil leaves.

Nutrition: Calories: 480, Total Fat: 22g, Saturated Fat: 6g, Cholesterol: 30mg, Sodium: 940mg, Total Carbohydrates: 54g, Dietary Fiber: 7g, Sugars: 7g, Protein: 19g

Mediterranean Roasted Mushrooms

Prep Time: 20 minutes **Cook time:** 30 minutes **Serving:** 2

Ingredients:
8 mushrooms
1 tablespoon olive oil
400g low-fat ricotta
1 zucchini, grated
4 shallots, finely diced
1/4 cup semidried tomatoes, chopped
25g pitted olives, chopped
1/4 cup basil leaves, roughly chopped
2 tablespoons pine nuts, toasted

1 egg, lightly beaten
100g baby rocket leaves
4 slices sourdough bread

Directions: Preheat your oven to 400°F (200°C). Place the mushrooms on a baking sheet and brush them with olive oil. Roast the mushrooms in the oven for 15 minutes, or until they are tender and caramelized. In a large mixing bowl, combine the grated zucchini, diced shallots, chopped semidried tomatoes, and olives. Stir in the ricotta cheese, basil, pine nuts, and egg until everything is combined. Divide the ricotta mixture among the roasted mushrooms. Return the mushrooms to the oven and bake for an additional 10-15 minutes, or until the mushrooms are heated through. Serve the roasted mushrooms, garnished with baby rocket leaves and accompanied by toasted sourdough bread.

Nutrition: Calories: 603, Total Fat: 37g, Saturated Fat: 17g, Cholesterol: 118mg, Sodium: 927mg, Total Carbohydrates: 47g, Dietary Fiber: 6g, Sugar: 7g, Protein: 25g

Chicken Thighs with Tahini Noodles

Prep Time: 10 minutes **Cook time:** 20 minutes **Serving:** 2

Ingredients:
1 tablespoon olive oil
8 chicken thighs
250g sliced banana
2 cloves garlic, crushed
150g tahini
12 lemons, juiced
23 tablespoons Ketjap manis
Chili flakes, to taste
300ml chicken stock
200g egg noodles

Directions: Heat the olive oil in a large skillet over medium heat. Add the chicken thighs and cook until they are browned on both sides and cooked through. Remove the chicken from the skillet and set aside. In the same skillet, add the sliced banana and cook until it is caramelized. Stir in the crushed garlic and cook for an additional minute. Add the tahini, lemon juice, ketjap manis, and chili flakes to the skillet and stir until everything is well combined. Gradually add the chicken stock to the skillet, stirring constantly until the sauce is smooth and thickened. Cook the egg noodles according to package instructions, then drain and add them to the skillet with the sauce. Gently toss the noodles with the sauce until they are well coated. Return the chicken thighs to the skillet and gently toss them with the noodles and sauce until they are heated through. Serve the chicken and noodles hot, garnished with fresh herbs or sesame seeds if desired.

Nutrition per serving: Calories: 817, Protein: 37 grams, Fat: 49 grams, Carbohydrates: 65 grams, Sugar: 21 grams, Fiber: 5 grams, Sodium: 1270 milligrams

Beef Stew with Eggplants

Preparation time: 15 minutes **Cooking time:** 10 hours **Servings:** 2

Ingredients:
10 oz beef neck or other tender cut, chopped into bite-sized pieces
1 large eggplant, sliced
2 cups fire-roasted tomatoes
1/2 cup fresh green peas
1 cup beef broth
4 tbsp olive oil
2 tbsp tomato paste
1 tbsp Cayenne pepper, ground
1/2 tsp chili pepper, ground (optional)
1/2 tsp salt
Parmesan cheese, grated (optional)

Directions: In a pot, heat the olive oil over medium heat. Add the beef and cook until it is browned on all sides. Stir in the tomato paste and cook for an additional minute. Add the sliced eggplant, fire-roasted tomatoes, green peas, beef broth, Cayenne pepper, chili pepper (if using), and salt to the pot. Stir until everything is well combined. Bring the stew to a simmer and reduce the heat to low. Cover the pot and simmer the stew for 8-10 hours. Serve the stew garnished with grated Parmesan cheese.

Nutrition per serving: Calories: 560, Fat: 40g, Saturated fat: 13g, Carbohydrates: 30g, Sugar: 13g, Protein: 30g, Fiber: 8g, Sodium: 880mg

Pepper Meat

Preparation time: 15 minutes **Cooking time:** 10 hours **Servings:** 6

Ingredients:
2 lbs beef fillet or other tender cut
5 medium-sized onions, peeled and finely chopped
3 tbsp tomato paste
2 tbsp oil
1 tbsp butter, melted
2 tbsp fresh parsley, finely chopped
1/2 tsp freshly ground black pepper
1 tsp salt

Directions: Preheat your oven to 350°F (180°C). In a large skillet, heat the oil over medium heat. Add the beef and cook until it is browned on all sides. Remove the beef from the skillet and set aside. In the same skillet, add the chopped onions and cook until they are soft and translucent. Stir in the tomato paste and cook for an additional minute. Add the melted butter, parsley, black pepper, and salt to the skillet and stir until everything is well combined. Place the beef in a baking dish and pour the onion mixture over the top. Cover the dish with aluminum foil and bake for 1 hour, or until the beef is tender and cooked through. Serve the pepper meat hot, garnished with fresh parsley.

Nutrition: Calories 382, Proteins 47.3g, Carbohydrates 10.3g, Fat 16g.

Winter Lamb Stew

Preparation time: 15 minutes **Cooking time**: 10 hours **Servings**: 4

Ingredients:
1 lb lamb neck, boneless
2 medium-sized potatoes, peeled and chopped into bite-sized pieces
2 large carrots, sliced
1 medium-sized tomato, diced
1 small red bell pepper, chopped
1 garlic head, whole
A handful of fresh parsley, finely chopped
2 tbsp extra virgin olive oil
1/4 cup lemon juice
1/2 tsp salt
1/2 tsp black pepper, ground

Directions: In a large pot, heat the olive oil over medium heat. Add the lamb neck and cook until it is browned on all sides. Add the chopped potatoes, sliced carrots, diced tomato, and chopped red bell pepper to the pot. Stir until everything is well combined. Add the whole garlic head, parsley, lemon juice, salt, and black pepper to the pot. Stir until everything is well combined. Bring the stew to a simmer and reduce the heat to low. Cover the pot and simmer the stew for 1 hour, or until the lamb is tender and the vegetables are cooked through. Remove the garlic head from the stew and discard it. Serve the stew hot, garnished with fresh parsley.

Nutrition: Calories 379, Proteins 34.6g, Carbohydrates 24.2g, Fat 15.7g

Spinach and Artichoke Frittata

Prep Time: 5 minutes **Cook time:** 20 minutes **Serving:** 8

Ingredients:
10 large eggs
1/2 cup full-fat sour cream
1 tablespoon Dijon mustard
1 teaspoon kosher salt
1/4 teaspoon black pepper
1 cup grated Parmesan cheese
2 tablespoons olive oil
14 ounces marinated artichoke hearts, drained and chopped
5 ounces baby spinach
2 minced garlic cloves

Directions: Preheat your oven to 350°F (180°C). In a bowl, whisk together the eggs, sour cream, Dijon mustard, salt, and black pepper until the mixture is combined. Stir in the grated Parmesan cheese. In a large oven-safe skillet, heat the olive oil over medium heat. Add the chopped artichoke hearts and cook until they are tender. Stir in the baby spinach and minced garlic and cook until the spinach is wilted. Pour the egg mixture into the skillet and stir until everything is combined. Transfer the skillet to the oven and bake the frittata for 20-25 minutes, or until it is set and the top is golden brown.

Nutrition: Calories: 227, Fat: 18.3g, Saturated fat: 7.5g, Carbohydrates: 8.5g, Sugar: 2.6g, Protein: 11.6g, Cholesterol: 244mg, Sodium: 616mg, Fiber: 2.4g

Smoked Salmon and Watercress Salad

Preparation time: 5 minutes **Cooking time:** 0 minutes **Servings:** 4

Ingredients:
2 bunches watercress
2 lbs smoked salmon, skinless, boneless, and flaked
2 tsp mustard
1/4 cup lemon juice
1/2 cup Greek yogurt
Salt and black pepper, to taste
1 large cucumber, sliced
2 tbsp chives, chopped

Directions: Wash the watercress and pat it dry with paper towels. In a bowl, combine the flaked smoked salmon, mustard, lemon juice, Greek yogurt, salt, and black pepper. Stir until everything is well combined. Add the sliced cucumber and chopped chives to the bowl and gently toss until everything is well coated with the dressing. Arrange the watercress on a serving platter and top it with the smoked salmon mixture. Serve the salad garnished with additional chopped chives if desired.

Nutrition per serving: Calories: 260, Fat: 14g, Protein: 25g, Carbohydrates: 14g, Fiber: 3g, Sodium: 690mg

Greek Peppers Stuffed Chicken

Prep time: 30 minutes **Cook time**: 0 minutes **Serving**: 6

Ingredients
2/3 cup Greek yogurt
2 tablespoons Dijon mustard
2 tablespoons seasoned rice vinegar
A pinch of kosher salt
A pinch of black pepper
1/3 cup chopped fresh parsley
1 rotisserie chicken, cubed
4 stalks celery, sliced
1 bunch scallions, thinly sliced
1 pint cherry tomatoes, halved
1/2 English cucumber, diced
3 bell peppers, seeded and cut into 1-inch pieces

Directions: In a bowl, combine the Greek yogurt, Dijon mustard, seasoned rice vinegar, salt, and black pepper. Stir until well combined. In another bowl, combine the cubed rotisserie chicken, sliced celery, scallions, cherry tomatoes, diced cucumber, and bell peppers. Stir until everything is well combined. Add the Greek yogurt mixture to the bowl and toss until everything is well coated. Divide the mixture evenly among the bell peppers and place them in a baking dish. Bake the peppers in a preheated 350°F (180°C) oven for 20-25 minutes, or until they are tender and the filling is heated through. Serve the Greek peppers stuffed chicken hot, garnished with additional chopped parsley if desired.

Nutrition per serving: Calories: 273, Total Fat: 13g, Saturated Fat: 4g, Cholesterol: 75mg, Sodium: 539mg, Carbohydrates: 20g, Fiber: 3g, Sugar: 10g, Protein: 23g

Salmon with Farro Dressing

Prep time: 10 minutes **Cook time:** 30 minutes**Serving**: 4

Ingredients
2 tablespoons tahini
1 lemon, zested and juiced
1/2 teaspoon turmeric

1/4 teaspoon garlic powder
6 tablespoons olive oil
A pinch of black pepper
A pinch of kosher salt
1/4 cup faro, cooked according to package instructions
1/2 cup cooked black beans
1/2 teaspoon cumin
6 ounces salmon
1 1/2 teaspoons smoked paprika
1/2 teaspoon coriander
4 Boston lettuce leaves
1/2 avocado, sliced
2 scallions, thinly sliced
1/4 Fresno chile, thinly sliced

Directions: In a small mixing bowl, combine the tahini, lemon zest, lemon juice, turmeric, garlic powder, olive oil, black pepper, and kosher salt. Stir until everything is well combined. In a large mixing bowl, combine the cooked faro, black beans, and cumin. Stir until everything is well combined. Place the salmon on a baking sheet and sprinkle it with the smoked paprika and coriander. Bake the salmon in a preheated 400°F (200°C) oven for 8-10 minutes, or until it is cooked through. Divide the Boston lettuce leaves among four plates and top them with the faro mixture, sliced avocado, scallions, and Fresno chile. Slice the baked salmon and place it on top of the salads. Drizzle the tahini dressing over the top of the salads and serve immediately.

Nutrition: Calories: 489, Fat: 33g, Saturated fat: 5g, Cholesterol: 48mg, Sodium: 286mg, Carbohydrates: 30g, Fiber: 7g, Sugar: 2g, Protein: 23g

Red Lentils Stew

Ready in about 50 minutes **Servings** 5

Ingredients:
2 tablespoons olive oil
2 medium carrots, chopped
1 celery, chopped
2 red bell peppers, sliced
1 yellow onion, chopped
1/2 teaspoon cumin
3 garlic cloves, minced
2 ripe tomatoes, pureed
2 tablespoons tomato paste
1 teaspoon dried rosemary
1/2 teaspoon dried thyme
5 cups vegetable broth, preferably homemade
Salt and pepper, to taste
1 tablespoon paprika
1 cup dry red lentils, rinsed
1/3 cup fresh cilantro, chopped

Directions: In a large pot, heat the olive oil over medium heat. Add the chopped carrots, celery, bell peppers, and onion to the pot. Cook until the vegetables are soft and translucent. Stir in the cumin, minced garlic, pureed tomatoes, tomato paste, rosemary, thyme, and paprika. Cook for an additional 2-3 minutes. Add the vegetable broth, salt, and pepper to the pot. Bring the stew to a simmer and reduce the heat to low. Add the rinsed lentils to the pot and simmer the stew for 20-30 minutes, or until the lentils are tender and the stew is thickened.

Nutrition: Calories 301; Fat 10.8g; Carbs 44g; Protein 14.1g; Sugars 7.5g

Mussels and Clams in White Wine

Preparation time: 10 minutes **Cooking time:** 10 minutes **Servings:** 4

Ingredients:
2 tablespoons extra-virgin olive oil
1 shallot, minced
2 garlic cloves, minced
1 cup dry white wine
1/2 teaspoon red pepper flakes
2 pounds clams, scrubbed
2 pounds mussels, scrubbed and debearded
1/4 cup chopped arugula

Directions: In a large pot, heat the olive oil over medium heat. Add the minced shallot and garlic to the pot and cook until they are soft and fragrant. Add the white wine, red pepper flakes, and clams to the pot. Bring the mixture to a boil and reduce the heat to low. Cover the pot and simmer for 5-6 minutes, or until the clams have opened. Add the mussels to the pot and cover it again. Simmer for an additional 3-4 minutes, or until the mussels have opened. Discard any clams or mussels that have not opened. Stir in the chopped arugula and serve the mussels and clams in white wine immediately.
Variation tip: serve this dish over linguine if you like.

Nutrition per serving: Calories: 314, Fat: 17.5g, Saturated Fat: 2.5g, Cholesterol: 78mg, Sodium: 556mg, Carbohydrates: 14.5g, Fiber: 2g, Sugar: 3.5g, Protein: 25g

Colorful Sardines Omelet

Ready in about 35 minutes **Servings** 2

Ingredients:
4 eggs, whisked
1/2 red bell pepper, sliced
1/2 green bell pepper, sliced
1/2 can sardines, drained and cut into small pieces
1/2 cup Monterey Jack cheese, shredded
1 tablespoon olive oil
1/3 teaspoon salt
1/4 teaspoon pepper

Directions: Heat the olive oil in a large pan over medium heat. Add the sliced bell peppers to the pan and cook until they are soft and caramelized. Add the sardines to the pan and cook for an additional 2-3 minutes. In a small mixing bowl, whisk together the eggs, salt, and pepper. Pour the egg mixture over the vegetables and sardines in the pan. Stir gently to combine. Sprinkle the shredded cheese over the top of the omelet. Reduce the heat to low and cook the omelet for an additional 5-7 minutes, or until the eggs are cooked through and the cheese is melted. Serve the omelet immediately, garnished with additional sliced bell peppers and sardines, if desired.

Nutrition: Calories 326; Fat 25.4g; Carbs 3.5g; Protein 20.4g; Sugars 1.9g

Classic Roasted Chicken

Cooking time 20 minutes **Servings** 3

Ingredients:
1 whole chicken
1/2 cup soy sauce
1 large red onion, sliced
1/3 cup fresh rosemary, finely chopped
1/3 cup freshly squeezed lemon juice
1/2 cup olive oil
2 teaspoons paprika
1/3 cup fresh thyme, finely chopped
1 celery, sliced
Sea salt and pepper, to taste
2 cups chicken broth

Directions: Preheat your oven to 350°F (180°C). In a mixing bowl, whisk together the soy sauce, lemon juice, olive oil, paprika, and thyme. Place the sliced red onion and celery in the bottom of a roasting pan. Place the whole chicken on top of the vegetables in the roasting pan. Brush the soy sauce mixture over the top of the chicken. Sprinkle the chicken with sea salt and pepper. Pour the chicken broth into the bottom of the roasting pan. Place the roasting pan in the preheated oven and roast the chicken for 1 1/2 hours, or until the internal temperature reaches 165°F (74°C). Let the chicken rest for 10 minutes before carving. Serve the roasted chicken with the vegetables and pan juices.

Nutrition: Calories 285; Fat 9.9g; Carbs 21.6g; Protein 27.1g; Sugars 12.2g

Pork Loin with Cilantro mustard Glaze

Servings: 4 **Cooking Time:35** Minutes

Ingredients:
2 tablespoons olive oil
1 onion, chopped
2 pounds pork loin, cut into strips
1/2 cup vegetable stock
Salt and black pepper to taste
2 teaspoons mustard
1 tablespoon cilantro, chopped

Directions: In a pan, heat the olive oil over medium heat. Add the chopped onion and pork loin strips to the pan and cook until the pork is browned on all sides. Add the vegetable stock to the pan and season the pork with salt and black pepper. Bring the mixture to a boil and then reduce the heat to low. Simmer the pork loin for 20-25 minutes, or until it is cooked through and tender. In a bowl, whisk together the mustard and cilantro. Brush the cilantro mustard glaze over the top of the cooked pork loin. Serve the pork loin with the cilantro mustard glaze, garnished with additional cilantro, if desired.
Nutrition per Serving: Calories: 300; Fat: 13g; Protein: 24g; Carbs: 15g.

Slow Cooker Beef with Tomatoes

Servings: 4 **Cooking Time:8** Hours 10 Minutes

Ingredients:
1 ½ lb beef shoulder, cubed
½ cup chicken stock
2 tomatoes, chopped
2 garlic cloves, minced

1 tbsp cinnamon powder
Salt and black pepper to taste
2 tbsp cilantro, chopped

Directions: Place the beef in the slow cooker. Pour in the chicken stock and add the tomatoes, garlic, and cinnamon powder. Season with salt and black pepper to taste. Cover the slow cooker and cook on low heat for 6-8 hours or until the beef is tender. Stir in the cilantro before serving. Serve over rice or with your choice of side dish.

Nutrition per Serving: Calories: 360; Fat: 16g; Protein: 16g; Carbs: 19g.

Sole Fillets with Lemon Sauce

Ready in about 20 minutes **Servings** 2

Ingredients:
3 tablespoons olive oil
1/3 teaspoon Kosher salt
4 tablespoons lemon juice
½ lb. petrale sole fillets
½ teaspoon oregano
Salt and pepper, to taste
4 tablespoons melted ghee

Directions: Preheat your oven to 400°F. In a small bowl, mix together the olive oil, Kosher salt, lemon juice, and oregano. Place the sole fillets in a baking dish and pour the lemon sauce over them. Season with salt and pepper to taste. Drizzle the melted ghee over the top of the fillets. Bake the fillets for 10-12 minutes, or until they are cooked through and flaky. Serve the fillets hot, garnished with additional lemon wedges and a sprinkle of oregano, if desired.

Nutrition: Calories 275; Fat 22.6g; Carbs 4.5g; Protein 14.5g; Sugars 2.3g

Pistachio Sole Fish

Preparation time: 4 minutes **Cooking time:** 11 minutes **Servings:** 4

Ingredients:
4 Boneless sole fillets
A pinch of Salt and pepper
½ c. pistachios, finely chopped
Zest of 1 lemon
Juice of 1 lemon
1 tsp extra virgin olive oil

Directions: Preheat your oven to 400°F. Season the sole fillets with a pinch of salt and pepper. In a small bowl, mix together the chopped pistachios, lemon zest, and lemon juice. Place the sole fillets in a baking dish and top them with the pistachio mixture. Drizzle the olive oil over the top of the fillets. Bake the fillets for 10-12 minutes, or until they are cooked through and flaky. Serve the fillets hot, garnished with additional lemon wedges and a sprinkle of chopped pistachios, if desired. Store in airtight containers in your fridge for 1–2 days.

Nutrition: Calories: 150, Fat: 8g, Cholesterol: 65mg, Sodium: 90mg, Carbohydrates: 4g, Protein: 17g

Mushroom and Potato Oat Burgers

Preparation time: 20 minutes **Cooking time:** 21 minutes **Servings:** 5

Ingredients:
½ cup minced onion
1 teaspoon grated fresh ginger
½ cup minced mushrooms
½ cup red lentils, rinsed
¾ sweet potato, peeled and diced
1 cup vegetable stock
2 tablespoons hemp seeds
2 tablespoons chopped parsley
2 tablespoons chopped cilantro
1 tablespoon curry
1 cup quick oats
Brown rice flour, optional
5 tomato slices
Lettuce leaves
5 wholewheat buns

Directions: In a saucepan, bring the vegetable stock to a boil. Add the minced onion, grated ginger, minced mushrooms, and red lentils. Reduce the heat to low and simmer for 20 minutes, or until the lentils are tender. In the meantime, steam the diced sweet potato until it is tender, about 8-10 minutes. In a bowl, mash the cooked sweet potato and add the lentil mixture, hemp seeds, chopped parsley, chopped cilantro, and curry. Add the quick oats to the mixture and mix until well combined. If the mixture is too wet, add some brown rice flour to help bind it together. Form the mixture into 5 patties. Heat a skillet over medium heat and add the patties. Cook for 5-6 minutes on each side, or until they are browned and heated through. Place a lettuce leaf on the bottom of each bun, followed by a tomato slice and a mushroom and potato oat patty. Top with the top half of the bun and serve.

Nutrition: Calories: 266, fat: 5.3g, protein: 14.5g, carbs: 48.7g, fiber: 9.6g, sodium: 276mg

Spanish Chicken Skillet

Servings:4 **Cooking Time:**25 Minutes

Ingredients:
2 tbsp olive oil
½ cup chicken stock
4 chicken breasts
2 garlic cloves, minced
1 celery stalk, chopped
1 tbsp oregano, dried
Salt and black pepper to taste
1 white onion, chopped
1 ½ cups tomatoes, cubed
10 green olives, sliced

Directions: In a skillet, heat the olive oil over medium heat. Add the chicken breasts to the skillet and cook for 6-8 minutes on each side, or until they are cooked through. Remove the chicken from the skillet and set it aside. In the same skillet, add the garlic, celery, and onion. Cook for 3-4 minutes, or until the vegetables are tender. Add the chicken stock, tomatoes, oregano, salt, and black pepper. Stir to combine. Nestle the cooked chicken breasts back into the skillet, along with the sliced green olives. Reduce the heat to low and simmer for an additional 5-10 minutes, or until the sauce has thickened slightly. Serve the chicken and vegetables, garnished with oregano and green olives, if desired.

Nutrition per Serving: Calories: 140; Fat: 7g; Protein: 11g; Carbs: 13g.

Shrimps in Tomato Sauce

Ready in about 40 minutes **Servings** 2

Ingredients:
1/4 cup olive oil
1/2 cup red onion, chopped
4 garlic cloves, minced
1 can Italian tomatoes, crushed
1 teaspoon smoked paprika
1 lb. shrimp, peeled and deveined
1 tablespoon capers
½ teaspoon Kosher salt
1 lemon, cut into wedges
1 tablespoon tomato puree

Directions: In a large skillet, heat the olive oil over medium heat. Add the red onion and garlic and cook for 3-4 minutes, or until the onion is translucent. Stir in the crushed Italian tomatoes, smoked paprika, and tomato puree. Bring the mixture to a simmer and add the peeled and deveined shrimp. Cook the shrimp for 2-3 minutes, or until they are pink and cooked through. Stir in the capers and season with Kosher salt to taste. Squeeze the lemon wedges over the top of the shrimp and serve hot.

Nutrition: Calories 470; Fat 28.5g; Carbs 9.2g; Protein 47g; Sugars 3.2g

Pan Seared Salmon and Asparagus

Prep Time: 5 minutes **Cooking Time:** 20 minutes **Additional Time:** 0 minutes **Total Time:** 25 minutes **Servings:** 4

Ingredients:
46 oz. of salmon fillets
8 trimmed asparagus spears
1 tsp. saltfree butter
1 shallot, minced
4 tsp. of lemon juice
1/4 cup of olive oil
1/2 tsp. Dijon mustard
Salt and pepper to taste
2 1/2 tsp. minced basil

Directions: Preheat your oven to 400°F. In a large oven-safe skillet, heat the butter over medium heat. Season the salmon fillets with salt and pepper to taste and place them in the skillet. Cook the salmon for 3-4 minutes on each side, or until it is golden brown and starting to flake. Remove the skillet from the heat and transfer the salmon to a plate. In the same skillet, place the trimmed asparagus spears and cook for 3-4 minutes, or until they are tender. In a small bowl, whisk together the minced shallot, lemon juice, olive oil, Dijon mustard, salt, and pepper. Pour the mixture over the asparagus in the skillet and toss to coat. Nestle the salmon fillets back into the skillet, along with any juices that have accumulated on the plate. Transfer the skillet to the oven and bake for an additional 8-10 minutes, or until the salmon is cooked through and the asparagus is tender. Garnish the salmon and asparagus with minced basil before serving.

Nutrition: Calories: 474, Fat: 32.5g, Saturated Fat: 6.5g, Cholesterol: 95mg, Sodium: 413mg, Carbohydrates: 12.5g, Fiber: 3g, Sugar: 3.5g, Protein: 35g

Preparation Time: 15 minutes **Cooking Time**: 20 minutes **Servings**: 1

Ingredients:
2 skinless, boneless chicken breasts (8 ounces each), halved
3 tablespoons extravirgin olive oil, divided
1 teaspoon lemon zest
¼ cup crumbled feta cheese
2 tablespoons chopped Kalamata olives
2 tablespoons lemon juice
1 clove garlic, grated
2 teaspoons chopped fresh oregano
½ teaspoon salt, divided
½ teaspoon ground pepper, divided
¾ cup wholewheat orzo
2 cups thinly sliced baby spinach
1 cup chopped cucumber
1 cup chopped tomato
¼ cup chopped red onion

Directions: Preheat your grill to medium-high heat. In a small bowl, mix together 1 tablespoon of olive oil, the lemon zest, feta cheese, Kalamata olives, lemon juice, grated garlic, oregano, ¼ teaspoon salt, and ¼ teaspoon pepper. Place the chicken breasts in a large resealable plastic bag and add the feta cheese mixture. Toss to coat the chicken evenly. Grill the chicken for 6-8 minutes on each side, or until it is cooked through. In the meantime, bring a medium saucepan of salted water to a boil. Add the orzo to the boiling water and cook for 8-10 minutes, or until it is tender. Drain the orzo and transfer it to a large mixing bowl. Add the sliced baby spinach, chopped cucumber, chopped tomato, and chopped red onion to the bowl with the orzo. In a small bowl, whisk together the remaining 2 tablespoons of olive oil, ¼ teaspoon salt, and ¼ teaspoon pepper. Pour the olive oil mixture over the orzo salad and toss to coat. Serve the grilled chicken with the orzo salad on the side.

Nutrition per serving: Calories: 761, Protein: 50g, Total Fat: 45g, Saturated Fat: 9g, Cholesterol: 143mg, Carbohydrates: 41g, Fiber: 6g, Sodium: 974mg

Slow Cooker Chicken & Chickpea Soup

Preparation Time: 15 minutes **Cooking Time**: 20 minutes **Servings**: 1

Ingredients:
1 ½ cups dried chickpeas, soaked overnight
4 cups water
¼ teaspoon ground pepper
2 pounds bonein chicken thighs
1 (14 ounces) can artichoke hearts, drained and quartered
¼ cup halved pitted oilcured olives
½ teaspoon salt
¼ cup chopped fresh parsley or cilantro
1 large yellow onion, finely chopped
1 (15 ounces) can nosalt-added diced tomatoes, preferably fireroasted
2 tablespoons tomato paste
4 cloves' garlic, finely chopped
1 bay leaf
4 teaspoons ground cumin
4 teaspoons paprika
¼ teaspoon cayenne pepper

Directions: Drain and rinse the soaked chickpeas. In a slow cooker, combine the chickpeas, water, ground pepper, chicken thighs, artichoke hearts, oil-cured olives, salt, parsley or cilantro, onion, diced tomatoes, tomato paste, garlic, bay leaf, cumin, paprika, and cayenne pepper. Cover the slow cooker and cook on low for 8-10 hours, or on high for 4 hours, or until the chicken is tender and falling off.

Nutrition: Calories: 635, Fat: 17g, Saturated fat: 4g, Cholesterol: 159mg, Sodium: 571mg, Carbohydrates: 71g, Fiber: 16g, Sugar: 13g, Protein: 53g

Slow Cooker Mediterranean Chicken & Orzo

Preparation Time: 15 minutes **Cooking Time**: 20 minutes **Servings**: 1

Ingredients:
1pound boneless, skinless chicken breasts, trimmed
1 cup low sodium chicken broth
2 medium tomatoes, chopped
1 medium onion, halved and sliced
⅓ cup quartered black or green olives
2 tablespoons chopped fresh parsley
Zest and juice of 1 lemon
1 teaspoon herb de Provence
½ teaspoon salt
½ teaspoon ground pepper
¾ cup wholewheat orzo

Directions: Place the chicken breasts in the base of a large slow cooker. In a medium mixing bowl, combine the chicken broth, chopped tomatoes, sliced onion, quartered olives, chopped parsley, lemon zest and juice, herb de Provence, salt, and pepper. Pour the mixture over the chicken breasts in the slow cooker. Cover the slow cooker and cook on low for 6-8 hours, or until the chicken is tender and cooked through. During the last 30 minutes of cooking, add the orzo to the slow cooker and stir to combine. Cover the slow cooker and continue cooking until the orzo is tender, about 20-30 minutes more. Serve the chicken and orzo hot, garnished with additional chopped pars.

Nutrition: Calories 437, protein 37g, carbohydrates 75g, fiber 5g, fat 4g, saturated fat 1g, sodium 591mg

DESSERTS

Mediterranean Parfait

Prep Time: 15 minutes **Servings**: 2

Ingredients:
1 mango
2 pomegranates
1/2 cup yogurt
2 pistachios

Directions: Slice the mango in half, then slice off the flesh from the pit. Dice the mango into small pieces. Cut the pomegranates in half and carefully remove the seeds. Set the seeds aside. In a small bowl, mix together the diced mango and pomegranate seeds. In a parfait glass, layer the yogurt, mango and pomegranate mixture, and yogurt again. Repeat the layering process until you reach the top of the glass. Garnish the top of the parfait with crushed pistachios.

Nutrition per serving: Calories: 150 Total fat: 4g Saturated fat: 2g Cholesterol: 10mg Sodium: 50mg Total carbohydrate: 26g Dietary fiber: 3g Sugar: 21g Protein: 5g

Almond Chocolate Mousse

Ready in about 15 minutes + chilling time **Servings** 4

Ingredients:
1/2 cup Greek yogurt
1/4 cup ghee, melted
1 cup bittersweet chocolate, chopped
1/2 cup brown sugar
A pinch of salt
1/2 teaspoon vanilla
3 tablespoons peeled almonds, finely chopped

Directions: In a small saucepan, melt the chocolate and ghee over low heat, stirring constantly until smooth. Remove the saucepan from the heat and stir in the brown sugar, salt, and vanilla. Let the chocolate mixture cool slightly, then stir in the Greek yogurt until well combined. Divide the chocolate mousse among four small bowls or cups and sprinkle with chopped almonds. Serve the chocolate mousse chilled or at room temperature, garnished with additional chopped almonds if desired.

Nutrition: Calories 257; Fat 1.6g; Carbs 58.2g; Protein 3.9g; Sugars 43g

Crepes

Prep Time: 10 minutes **Cooking Time:** 10 minutes **Servings:** 4

Ingredients:
1 cup flour
4 eggs
1 1/3 cups milk
2 tbsp. butter
2 tbsp. sugar
1/2 tsp. salt

Directions: In a medium mixing bowl, whisk together the flour, eggs, milk, butter, sugar, and salt until smooth. Heat a crepe pan or large nonstick skillet over medium heat. Lightly coat the pan with cooking spray. Pour about ¼ cup of the crepe batter into the pan and quickly swirl the pan to spread the batter evenly. Cook the crepe for 1-2 minutes, or until the edges start to turn golden. Carefully flip the crepe and cook for an additional 1-2 minutes, or until the second side is golden. Repeat the process with the remaining crepe batter, lightly coating the pan with cooking spray between each crepe. Serve the crepes hot, garnished with your desired toppings.

Nutrition: Calories: 178, Fat: 10g, Saturated Fat: 5g, Cholesterol: 162mg, Sodium: 240mg, Carbohydrates: 18g, Fiber: 1g, Sugar: 7g, Protein: 6g.

Cashew and Peanut Rice Pudding

Serves: 4 **Planning Time:** 5 minutes **Cook Time:** 55 minutes

Ingredients:
2 cups skim milk
1 cup hefty cream
1 cup brown rice, flushed
1/3 cup natural vanished milk
½ cup toasted cashews and pecans squashed

2 tsp vanilla concentrate
2 tsp cinnamon powder
3 tbsp sugar
2 tbsp butter, temperature
Date syrup for garnish

Directions: In a medium saucepan, bring the skim milk, heavy cream, and brown rice to a boil over medium heat. Reduce the heat to low and simmer for 20-25 minutes, or until the rice is tender and the pudding has thickened. Stir in the evaporated milk, toasted cashews and pecans, vanilla extract, cinnamon, and sugar. Cook for an additional 5 minutes, stirring constantly. Remove the pudding from heat and stir in the melted butter. Transfer the pudding to a serving dish and garnish with date syrup, if desired. Serve the pudding warm or chilled.

Nutrition: Calories 646, Fats 39.77g, Carbs 62.14g, Net Carbs 58.74g, Protein 12.69g

Super Simple Pears

Time: 25 minutes + chilling time **Servings:** 6

Ingredients:
1/2 cup honey
½ teaspoon cinnamon
½ teaspoon vanilla
6 pears
1/3 cup pecan, chopped

Directions: Preheat your oven to 350°F (180°C). In a bowl, mix together the honey, cinnamon, and vanilla. Set aside. Slice the pears into wedges and arrange them in a single layer on a baking sheet. Drizzle the honey mixture over the pear wedges, making sure to coat them evenly. Sprinkle the chopped pecans over the top of the pears. Bake the pears in the preheated oven for 15-20 minutes, or until they are tender and caramelized. Let the pears cool slightly before serving.

Nutrition: Calories 254; Fat 4.7g; Carbs 57.2g; Protein 1.4g; Sugars 5.8g

Macadamia Nut Cookies

Prep Time: 30 minutes **Cooking Time:** 10 minutes **Total Time:** 40 minutes **Servings:** 6

Ingredients:
1 1/2 cup macadamia nuts
4 oz. butter
1 1/2 tsp. vanilla extract
1 large egg
2 cups flour
1 3/4 cup chocolate chips
1 tsp. baking soda
3/4 cup shortening vegetable
1/2 cup brown sugar
1/2 cup sugar

Directions: Preheat your oven to 350°F (180°C) and line a baking sheet with parchment paper. In a food processor, pulse the macadamia nuts until they are finely chopped. Set aside. In a large mixing bowl, cream together the butter, shortening, brown sugar, and sugar until light and fluffy. Beat in the egg and vanilla extract. In a separate bowl, whisk together the flour and baking soda. Gradually add this to the butter mixture, mixing until well combined. Stir in the chopped macadamia nuts and chocolate chips. Drop spoonfuls of the cookie dough onto the prepared baking sheet, leaving about 2 inches of space between each cookie. Bake the cookies in the preheated oven for 10-12 minutes, or until they are golden brown around the edges. Remove the cookies from the oven and let them cool on the baking sheet for a few minutes before transferring them to a wire rack to cool completely.

Nutrition per serving: Calories: 564, Fat: 37g, Saturated Fat: 14g, Cholesterol: 60mg, Sodium: 359mg, Carbohydrates: 57g, Fiber: 2g, Sugar: 35g, Protein: 7g

Pumpkin yoghurt parfait

Serves: 4 **Planning Time:** 5 minutes **Chilling Time:** halfhour

Ingredients:
1 (15 oz) can pumpkin puree
1 1/4 cups Greek yogurt
1 tsp vanilla extract
2 tbsp date syrup
2 1/2 tbsp coconut sugar
A pinch of nutmeg
2 tsp cinnamon
A small handful of pecans, for decorating (optional)

Directions: In a medium bowl, mix together the pumpkin puree, Greek yogurt, vanilla extract, date syrup, coconut sugar, nutmeg, and cinnamon until well combined. Spoon the pumpkin yogurt mixture into individual serving glasses or bowls. Top each parfait with a sprinkle of pecans and serve chilled.

Nutrition: Calories 418, Fats 25.63g, Carbs 36.77g, Net Carbs 28.57g, Protein 15.6g

Greek Yogurt with Goji Berries and strawberries

Preparation time: 3 minutes **Servings:** 1

Ingredients:
A handful of strawberries, sliced
A handful of Goji berries
2 tbsp Greek yogurt

Directions: In a small bowl, mix together the Greek yogurt and Goji berries. Top the mixture with the sliced strawberries. Serve the yogurt immediately. **Note:** You can also add other toppings to this recipe, such as chopped nuts, granola, or a drizzle of honey. The possibilities are endless!

Nutrition: Calories: 119, Fat: 2g, Sodium: 29mg, Carbohydrates: 18g, Fiber: 2g, Sugar: 12g, Protein: 9g

Yellow Cake

Prep Time: 15 minutes **Cooking Time:** 30 minutes **Additional Time:** 0 minutes **Total Time:** 45 minutes **Servings:** 6

Ingredients:
1 3/4 cups all-purpose flour
2 tsp baking powder
1/4 tsp salt
3/4 cup unsalted butter, softened
1 cup granulated sugar
3 large eggs
1 tsp vanilla extract
1 cup milk

Directions: Preheat your oven to 350°F (180°C) and grease a 9x9 inch square baking pan. In a medium bowl, whisk together the flour, baking powder, and salt. Set aside. In a large mixing bowl, beat the butter and sugar together until light and fluffy. Add the eggs, one at a time, beating well after each addition. Stir in the vanilla extract. Add the dry ingredients to the butter mixture in three parts, alternating with the milk and beginning and ending with the dry ingredients. Mix until just combined. Pour the batter into the prepared baking pan and smooth the top with a spatula. Bake the cake in the preheated oven for 25-30 minutes, or until a toothpick inserted into the center comes out clean. Let the cake cool in the pan for a few minutes before transferring it to a wire rack to cool completely. Serve the cake plain or topped with your favorite frosting.

Nutrition: Calories: 357, Fat: 18g, Saturated Fat: 11g, Cholesterol: 104mg, Sodium: 198mg, Carbohydrates: 45g, Fiber: 1g, Sugar: 27g, Protein: 6g

Cherry-Peach Compote with Greek Yoghurt

Serves: 4 **Planning Time:** 10 minutes + 1 hour cooling time **Cook Time**: 5 minutes
Ingredients:
4 peaches, divided and thinly sliced
1 lb cherries, pitted and divided
2 cups wine
3/4 cup coconut sugar
1 1/2 cups Greek yogurt
1 tsp cinnamon
1 tsp vanilla extract
1 tbsp date syrup

Directions: In a large saucepan, bring the wine and coconut sugar to a boil over medium heat. Add half of the sliced peaches and half of the pitted cherries to the wine mixture. Reduce the heat to low and simmer for 15-20 minutes, or until the fruit is tender and the compote has thickened. Remove the compote from the heat and stir in the cinnamon, vanilla, and date syrup. Let the compote cool for a few minutes before stirring in the remaining sliced peaches and pitted cherries. To serve, spoon the compote over a bowl of Greek yogurt.

Nutrition: Calories 193, Fats 0.4g, Carbs 41.01g, Net Carbs 39.11g, Protein 8.07g

Chocolate Fondue

Preparation Time: 5 minutes **Cooking Time:** 10 minutes **Servings:** 2
Ingredients:
1 cup water
½ tsp. sugar
½ cup coconut cream
¾ cup dark chocolate, chopped

Directions: In a small saucepan, bring the water and sugar to a boil over medium heat. Reduce the heat to low and add the coconut cream and dark chocolate. Stir constantly until the chocolate is melted and the mixture is smooth. Transfer the chocolate fondue to a fondue pot or small slow cooker to keep it warm. Serve the fondue with an assortment of fruit, cookies, and other treats for dipping.

Nutrition: Calories: 216 Fat: 17 g Carbs: 11 g Protein: 2 g

Greek Yogurt with Berries and Seeds

Preparation time: 3 minutes **Servings:** 1

Ingredients:
A handful of blueberries
A handful of raspberries
1 tbsp. Greek yogurt
1 tsp. sunflower seeds
1 tsp. pumpkin seeds
1 tsp. sliced almonds

Directions: In a small bowl, mix together the Greek yogurt and a selection of your favorite berries. Top the mixture with a sprinkle of sunflower seeds, pumpkin seeds, and sliced almonds.

Nutrition: Calories: 120 Total Fat: 7g Saturated Fat: 2g Cholesterol: 15mg Sodium: 20mg Total Carbohydrates: 13g Dietary Fiber: 2g Sugars: 9g Protein: 4g

One Ingredient Watermelon Sorbet

Preparation Time: 15 minutes **Cooking Time:** 20 minutes **Servings:** 1

Ingredients:
One medium ripe watermelon, peeled, cubed, and seeded

Directions: Place the cubed watermelon in a blender or food processor and blend until smooth. Pour the watermelon puree into a shallow dish or loaf pan and freeze for at least 4 hours, or until solid. To serve, use an ice cream scoop or spoon to scoop out the sorbet and place it in a bowl or cone. **Note:** If you prefer a sweeter sorbet, you can add a tablespoon or two of sugar to the watermelon puree before freezing. You can also add other flavors to the sorbet, such as mint or lime juice, if desired.

Nutrition: One cup of diced watermelon contains approximately 46 calories, 0.2g fat, 11g carbohydrate, 1g protein, and 0.6g fiber.

Lemon Curd

Preparation Time: 10 minutes **Cooking Time:** 10 minutes **Servings:** 2

Ingredients:
4 tbsp. butter
1 cup sugar
2/3 cup lemon juice
3 eggs
2 tsp. lemon zest
2 cups of water

Directions: In a medium saucepan, melt the butter over medium heat. Add the sugar, lemon juice, eggs, and lemon zest to the saucepan and whisk until combined. Cook the lemon curd over medium heat, stirring constantly, until it thickens and coats the back of a spoon. This will take about 10-15 minutes. Remove the lemon curd from the heat and let it cool to room temperature. Transfer the lemon curd to a jar or container with a tight-fitting lid and store it in the refrigerator until use.

Nutrition: Calories: 45, Fat: 1 g, Carbs: 8 g, Protein: 1 g

Red Wine Infused Pear

Prep time: 10 minutes **Cook time:** 25 minutes **Serves** 2

Ingredients:
2 firm pears, peeled
2 cups red wine

1 bay leaf
1 cinnamon stick
2 peppercorns
3 cardamom pods, split

Directions: In a medium saucepan, bring the red wine, bay leaf, cinnamon stick, peppercorns, and cardamom pods to a boil over medium heat. Reduce the heat to low and add the peeled pears to the wine mixture. Simmer for 15-20 minutes, or until the pears are tender. Remove the pears from the heat and let them cool in the wine mixture for a few minutes before transferring them to a serving dish. Serve the pears warm or chilled. **TIP:** If you enjoy apple more, then you can replace the pears to apples, or other fruits varying the time of simmering depending on their consistency.

Nutrition: Calories: 159, total fat: 12.0g, total carbs: 26.0g, sugar: 14.0g, protein: 1.0g, sodium: 24mg

Chocolate Truffles

Preparation time: 10 minutes **Cooking time:** 5 minutes **Makes** 16

Ingredients:
1/4 cup full-fat coconut milk
5 oz sugar-free dark chocolate, finely chopped
1 tbsp solid coconut oil, at room temperature
1/4 cup unsweetened cocoa powder, for coating

Directions: In a saucepan, bring the coconut milk to a boil over medium heat. Reduce the heat to low and add the dark chocolate and coconut oil. Stir constantly until the chocolate is melted and the mixture is smooth. Remove the chocolate mixture from the heat and let it cool for a few minutes. Once the chocolate has cooled slightly, use a small spoon or cookie scoop to portion out the mixture into small balls. Place the balls on a parchment-lined baking sheet. Refrigerate the truffles for at least 2 hours, or until firm. Once the truffles are firm, roll them in the cocoa powder to coat them evenly. Serve the truffles chilled.

Nutrition: calories: 75, fat: 6.0g, protein: 2.0g, carbs: 3.0g, net carbs: 1.0g, fiber: 2.0g

Strawberries Coated with Chocolate Chips

Preparation time: 10 minutes **Cooking time:** 5 minutes **Makes** 15

Ingredients:
5 oz sugar-free dark chocolate chips
1 tbsp vegetable shortening or lard
15 medium strawberries, fresh or frozen

Directions: In a small saucepan, melt the chocolate chips and vegetable shortening or lard over low heat, stirring constantly until the mixture is smooth. Dip the strawberries into the melted chocolate, turning them to coat them evenly. Place the chocolate-coated strawberries on a parchment-lined baking sheet. Refrigerate the strawberries for at least 2 hours, or until the chocolate has hardened. Serve the strawberries chilled.

Nutrition: calories: 216, fat: 18.0g, protein: 4.0g, carbs: 11.0g, net carbs: 6.0g, fiber: 5.0g

Rosé Poached Pears with Ginger and Vanilla

Preparation Time: 15 minutes **Cooking Time:** 20 minutes **Servings:** 1

Ingredients:
1 vanilla bean, split lengthwise

6 pears, peeled
Whipped cream, for serving
1 bottle dry rosé wine
1/2 cup sugar
1 inch piece fresh ginger, peeled

Directions: In a large saucepan, bring the rosé wine, sugar, and ginger to a boil over medium heat. Reduce the heat to low and add the vanilla bean and pears to the wine mixture. Simmer for 15-20 minutes, or until the pears are tender. Remove the pears from the heat and let them cool in the wine mixture for a few minutes before transferring them to a serving dish. Serve the pears warm or chilled, topped with a dollop of whipped cream.

Nutrition: calories: 1094, fat: 5.6g, carbohydrates: 70.9g, protein: 3.3g

Chocolate Glaze

Prep Time: 5 minutes **Cooking Time:** 5 minutes **Total Time:** 10 minutes **Servings:** 4

Ingredients:
1 oz. chocolate
2 tbsp. butter
4 1/2 oz. sugar
2 tbsp. water

Directions: In a saucepan, melt the chocolate and butter over low heat, stirring constantly until the mixture is smooth. Add the sugar and water to the saucepan and bring the mixture to a boil over medium heat. Reduce the heat to low and simmer the glaze for 2-3 minutes, or until it has thickened slightly. Remove the glaze from the heat and let it cool for a few minutes before use. **Note**: You can also add other flavors to this chocolate glaze, such as vanilla extract, peppermint extract, or instant coffee. Just be sure to add them to the saucepan along with the sugar and water.

Nutrition: Calories: 97, Total Fat: 7 g, Saturated Fat: 4 g, Cholesterol: 20 mg, Sodium: 41 mg, Total Carbohydrates: 11 g, Dietary Fiber: 1 g, Sugar: 10 g, Protein: 1 g

Chocolate brownies with Raspberry sauce

Prep Time: 10 minutes **Cook time:** 35 minutes **Serves** 2

RASPBERRY SAUCE:
1 cup frozen raspberries
¼ cup balsamic vinegar
BROWNIE:
2 tablespoons olive oil, divided
1 large egg
½ cup black beans with no added salt, rinsed
½ teaspoon vanilla extract
4 tablespoons unsweetened cocoa powder
¼ teaspoon baking powder
¼ cup sugar
Salt, to taste
¼ cup dark chocolate chips, plus more for topping
2 8ounce (227g) ramekins

Directions: Preheat your oven to 350°F (180°C). To make the raspberry sauce, place the frozen raspberries, balsamic vinegar, and 1 tablespoon of olive oil in a small saucepan. Cook over medium heat for 5-7 minutes, or until the raspberries are soft and the sauce has thickened. Set the sauce aside. To make the brownies, place the egg, black beans, vanilla, cocoa powder, baking powder, sugar, a pinch of salt, and the remaining oil in a blender or food processor. Blend until the mixture is smooth. Divide the brownie mixture evenly between the two ramekins. Top each ramekin with a sprinkle of chocolate chips. Bake the brownies for 20-25 minutes, or until they are firm to the touch. Serve the brownies warm, topped with a spoonful of raspberry sauce and a sprinkle of chocolate chips. **TIP:** Homemade salted caramel, custard, ganache are also good choices for topping. You can even top the brownies with chopped fresh fruits.

Nutrition: Calories: 512, total fat: 15.8g, cholesterol: 95mg, total carbs: 88.2g, fiber: 14.2g, sugar: 64.3g, protein: 10.1g, sodium: 123mg

Dessert platter

Preparation Time: 10 minutes **Cooking Time**: 15 minutes **Servings**: 1

Ingredients:
Iced doughnuts, to serve
50g baking chocolate (dark, white, or milk)
250g fresh cherries, washed and dried
250g cream cheese, chopped and at room temperature
125g sour cream
1 1/2 tbsp brown sugar
60ml Irish cream liqueur
200g dark chocolate, finely chopped
125ml pouring cream
100g chocolate brownies, broken into small chunks
1 tbsp chopped pecans or walnuts
Melted white chocolate, for drizzling

Directions: Start by melting the chocolate in a microwave-safe bowl according to the package instructions. Once the chocolate has melted, use a spoon or a pastry brush to coat the doughnuts with the chocolate. Place the chocolate-coated doughnuts on a plate or tray and refrigerate until the chocolate has hardened. In a medium bowl, mix together the cream cheese, sour cream, brown sugar, and Irish cream liqueur until smooth. In a separate bowl, melt the dark chocolate and cream together in the microwave according to the package instructions. Once the chocolate has melted, use a spoon or a pastry brush to coat the cherries with the chocolate mixture. Place the chocolate-coated cherries on a plate or tray and refrigerate until the chocolate has hardened. To assemble the dessert platter, arrange the chocolate-coated doughnuts, cherries, chocolate brownie chunks, and nuts on a large serving platter. Drizzle the white chocolate over the top of the platter, and serve immediately.

Nutrition (minus the iced doughnuts): Calories: 2944, Fat: 242g, Carbohydrates: 238g, Protein: 61g

Mini dessert calzones

Preparation Time: 10 minutes **Cooking Time**: 15 minutes **Servings**: 1

Ingredients:
250g fresh pizza dough
1 tablespoon Wonka Nerds rainbow
12 fresh raspberries
40g popping candy chocolate
Icing sugar, to serve (5g)

Directions: Preheat your oven to 400°F (200°C). Divide the pizza dough into 12 small balls. On a lightly floured surface, roll each ball of dough into a thin circle. Arrange the Wonka Nerds, raspberries, and popping candy chocolate in the center of each dough circle. Fold the dough circles in half to enclose the filling, pressing the edges to seal. Place the calzones on a baking sheet and bake for 10-12 minutes, or until the dough is golden brown and the filling is hot. Remove the calzones from the oven and let them cool for a few minutes before serving. Dust the calzones with icing sugar.

Nutrition per serving: Calories: 120 Total fat: 3.5g Saturated fat: 1.5g Cholesterol: 15mg Sodium: 120mg Total carbohydrate: 19g Dietary fiber: 1g Sugar: 6g Protein: 3g

Raspberry Compote

Preparation Time: 11 minutes **Cooking Time:** 30 minutes **Servings:** 2

Ingredients:
1 cup raspberries
½ cup Swerve
1 tsp freshly grated lemon zest
1 tsp vanilla extract
2 cups water

Directions: In a medium saucepan, bring the water to a boil over medium heat. Add the raspberries, Swerve, lemon zest, and vanilla extract to the saucepan. Reduce the heat to low and simmer the mixture for 5-7 minutes, or until the raspberries are soft and the compote has thickened. Remove the compote from the heat and let it cool for a few minutes before serving. Enjoy the compote over pancakes, waffles, ice cream, or any other dessert of your choice.

Nutrition: Calories: 48 Fat: 0.5 g Carbs: 5 g Protein: 1 g

FISH & SEAFOOD

Tomato-Basil Fish

Total Time 15 minutes **Servings** 2

Ingredients:
2 tsp grated Parmesan cheese
8 oz haddock fillets, red snapper, or cod
1/4 tsp dried basil
2 plum tomatoes, thinly sliced
1/8 tsp salt
1 tsp extra-virgin olive oil
1 tbsp lemon juice
1/8 tsp pepper

Directions: Preheat your oven to 400°F (200°C). Place the fish fillets in a baking dish and top them with the sliced tomatoes. In a small bowl, mix together the Parmesan cheese, basil, salt, olive oil, lemon juice, and pepper. Spread the cheese mixture over the top of the fish and tomatoes. Bake the fish for 15-20 minutes, or until it is cooked through and flakes easily with a fork. Serve the fish hot, garnished with additional basil or Parmesan cheese, if desired.

Nutrition per serving: Calories: 183, Fat: 9g, Cholesterol: 58mg, Sodium: 311mg, Carbohydrates: 7g, Protein: 20g

Salmon and Broccoli

Preparation time: 20 minutes **Cooking time:** 23 minutes **Servings:** 4

Ingredients
2 tbsp balsamic vinegar
1 broccoli head, florets separated
4 skinless salmon fillets
1 large red onion, roughly chopped
1 tbsp olive oil
Sea salt and black pepper, to taste

Directions: Preheat your oven to 400°F (200°C). Place the broccoli florets in a baking dish and top them with the salmon fillets. Scatter the red onion over the top of the salmon and broccoli. Drizzle the balsamic vinegar and olive oil over the top of the vegetables and fish. Season the salmon and broccoli with sea salt and black pepper, to taste. Bake the salmon and broccoli for 20-25 minutes, or until the fish is cooked through and the broccoli is tender. Serve the salmon and broccoli hot, garnished with additional balsamic vinegar or olive oil, if desired.

Nutrition: Calories 302, Fat 15.5g, Fiber 8.5g, Carbs 18.9g, Protein 19.8g

Mussels Bowls

Preparation time: 20 minutes **Cooking time:** 10 minutes **Servings:** 4

Ingredients:
2 lbs mussels, scrubbed
1 tbsp garlic, minced
1 tbsp basil, chopped
1 yellow onion, chopped
6 tomatoes, cubed
1 cup heavy cream
2 tbsp olive oil
1 tbsp parsley, chopped

Directions: In a saucepan, heat the olive oil over medium heat. Add the garlic and onion to the saucepan and cook for 2-3 minutes, or until the onion is translucent. Add the mussels to the saucepan and toss them in the garlic and onion mixture. Pour in the heavy cream and bring the mixture to a boil. Reduce the heat to low and simmer the mussels for 5-7 minutes, or until they are cooked through. Remove the mussels from the heat and stir in the basil and parsley. Divide the mussels among bowls, and top each bowl with the cubed tomatoes. Garnish with additional basil or parsley, if desired.

Nutrition: Calories 266, Fat 11.8g, Fiber 5.8g, Carbs 16.5g, Protein 10.5g

Grilled Tuna

Preparation time: 6 minutes **Cooking time:** 5 minutes **Servings:** 3

Ingredients:
3 tuna fillets
3 tsp teriyaki sauce
1/2 tsp minced garlic
1 tsp olive oil

Directions: Preheat your grill to high heat. In a bowl, mix together the teriyaki sauce, minced garlic, and olive oil. Place the tuna fillets in a shallow dish and brush them with the teriyaki mixture. Place

the tuna on the grill and cook for 3-4 minutes on each side, or until it is cooked to your desired level of doneness. Garnish with additional teriyaki sauce or minced garlic, if desired.
Nutrition: Calories 382, Fat 32.6g, Fiber 0g, Carbs 1.1g, Protein 21.4g

Healthy fish cakes

Preparation Time: 10 minutes **Cooking Time:** 15 minutes **Servings:** 1

Ingredients:
300g broccoli, cut into florets
400g skinless firm white fish fillets, chopped
400g can butter beans, rinsed and drained
1 tbsp wholegrain mustard
2 tbsp chopped fresh dill
2 tbsp chopped fresh continental parsley leaves
2 tsp finely grated lemon rind
90g (1 cup) rolled oats
1 tbsp extra virgin olive oil
120g mixed salad leaves
1/2 avocado, chopped
Lemon wedges, for serving

Directions: Preheat your oven to 400°F (200°C). Pulse the broccoli, fish, butter beans, mustard, dill, parsley, and lemon rind until the mixture is evenly combined. Transfer the mixture to a bowl and stir in the oats. Using your hands, shape the mixture into 8 patties. Place the patties on a baking sheet and brush them with the olive oil. Bake the fish cakes for 15-20 minutes, or until they are golden brown and cooked through. Garnish with the mixed salad leaves, avocado, and lemon wedges.

Nutrition: Calories: 250 Fat: 8g Saturated Fat: 1.5g Cholesterol: 45mg Sodium: 220mg Carbohydrates: 29g Fiber: 7g Sugar: 2g Protein: 18g

Fish and chickpea stew

Preparation Time: 10 minutes **Cooking Time:** 15 minutes **Servings:** 1

Ingredients:
1 brown onion, finely chopped
1 carrot, peeled and finely chopped
2 garlic cloves, crushed
400g can diced tomatoes
2 cups (500ml) fish stock
400g can chickpeas
500g firm white fish fillets
4 kale leaves
Finely grated Parmesan

Directions: In a saucepan, heat some oil over medium heat. Add the onion, carrot, and garlic to the saucepan and cook for 2-3 minutes, or until the vegetables are tender. Add the diced tomatoes, fish stock, and chickpeas to the saucepan and bring the mixture to a boil. Reduce the heat to low and simmer the stew for 10-15 minutes, or until the vegetables are tender. Add the fish fillets to the stew and cook for 5-7 minutes, or until they are cooked through. Add the kale to the stew and cook for an additional 2-3 minutes, or until it is wilted. Garnish with grated Parmesan, if desired.

Nutrition: Calories: 281, Fat: 9g, Carbohydrates: 25g, Protein: 31g, Sodium: 824mg

Baja Fish Tacos

Total Time 15 minutes **Difficulty Level** low **Servings** 2

Ingredients:
1 lb fresh cod
Salt and pepper, to taste
1 1/2 cups flour
1/2 tsp chili powder
1/2 tsp paprika
1/2 tsp garlic powder
1/2 tsp cumin
1/2 tsp salt
1/4 tsp pepper
12 oz beer (or sprite)
Oil, for frying

Directions: Cut the cod into small bite-sized pieces and season them with salt and pepper. In a shallow dish, mix together the flour, chili powder, paprika, garlic powder, cumin, salt, and pepper. Pour the beer (or sprite) into a separate shallow dish. Dip the cod pieces into the beer (or sprite), then coat them in the flour mixture. Heat some oil in a large frying pan over medium-high heat. Carefully add the coated cod pieces to the pan and cook them for 2-3 minutes on each side, or until they are golden brown and cooked through. Remove the cod from the pan and drain it on a paper towel. Serve the cod hot, in soft tacos or tortillas, garnished with your favorite taco toppings.

Nutrition: Calories: 598, Fat: 21g, Sodium: 812mg, Carbohydrates: 73g, Protein: 24g

Swordfish With Lemon and Tarragon

Prep time: 5 minutes **Cook time:** 15 minutes **Serves** 4

Ingredients:
1 pound (454 g) swordfish steaks, cut into 2inch pieces 1 teaspoon salt, or more to taste
¼ teaspoon freshly ground black pepper
¼ cup olive oil and plus 2 tablespoons, divided
2 tablespoons unsalted butter
2 tablespoons fresh tarragon, chopped
Zest and juice of 1 lemon
Zest and juice of 2 clementines

Directions: Preheat your grill to high heat. Season the swordfish steaks with the salt and black pepper. In a small bowl, mix together 1/4 cup of olive oil, the butter, tarragon, lemon zest and juice, and clementine zest and juice. Brush the swordfish steaks with the olive oil mixture. Place the swordfish on the grill and cook for 2-3 minutes on each side, or until it is cooked to your desired level of doneness. Remove the swordfish from the grill and let it rest for a few minutes. Serve the swordfish hot, garnished with additional tarragon, lemon zest, and clementine zest, if desired.

Nutrition: Calories: 383, total fat: 31.2g, saturated fat: 7.5g, total carbs: 3.2g, fiber: 0g, protein: 23.2g, sodium: 726mg

Healthy fish nacho bowl

Preparation Time: 10 minutes **Cooking Time:** 15 minutes **Servings:** 1

Ingredients:
500g white fish fillets (such as flathead), cut into 4-5cm pieces
2-3 tsp gluten-free chipotle seasoning or Mexican chili powder, to taste

1 tbsp extra virgin olive oil
400g red cabbage
425g can black beans, rinsed and drained
200g cherry tomatoes, halved
3 green shallots, thinly sliced
1 tbsp Greek-style yogurt
1/3 cup fresh coriander leaves
1 large lime, rind finely grated
1 small avocado
50g gluten-free corn chips

Directions: Preheat your grill to high heat. Season the fish fillets with the chipotle seasoning or Mexican chili powder. Brush the fish fillets with the olive oil. Place the fish on the grill and cook for 2-3 minutes on each side, or until it is cooked to your desired level of doneness. Remove the fish from the grill and let it rest for a few minutes. Meanwhile, divide the red cabbage, black beans, cherry tomatoes, and green shallots among four serving bowls. Top each bowl with a piece of grilled fish and a dollop of Greek-style yogurt. Garnish the bowls with fresh coriander, lime rind, and avocado slices. Serve the bowls hot, with gluten-free corn chips on the side.

Nutrition: Calories: 472, Protein: 34g, Carbohydrates: 46g, Fiber: 14g, Fat: 20g, Sodium: 651mg

Tasty COD Fish Balls

Total Time 25 minutes **Difficulty Level** low **Servings** 8

Ingredients:
1 cup all-purpose flour
3/4 cup parmesan cheese, grated
1 clove garlic, crushed
1 1/2 lbs cod fillets
2 tbsp olive oil
1 whole egg
1/4 cup parsley, fresh
1/2 tsp sea salt
3.5 oz whole wheat bread, sliced (crust removed)
1/4 tsp freshly ground black pepper

Directions: In a food processor, pulse the flour, parmesan cheese, garlic, cod fillets, olive oil, egg, parsley, sea salt, and whole wheat bread until the mixture is combined and forms a smooth dough. Roll the dough into small balls, about the size of a golf ball. Heat a large skillet over medium-high heat and add a little bit of oil. Add the fish balls to the skillet and cook for 3-4 minutes on each side, or until they are golden brown and cooked through. Remove the fish balls from the skillet and let them rest for a few minutes. Garnish with additional parsley and a sprinkle of black pepper, if desired.

Nutrition per serving: Calories: 260, Protein: 26g, Carbohydrates: 21g, Fat: 9g, Saturated fat: 3g, Cholesterol: 48mg, Sodium: 590mg, Fiber: 2g

Quick Mussels with White Wine Sauce

Prep time: 5 minutes **Cook time:** 10 minutes **Serves** 4

Ingredients:
2 pounds (907 g) small mussels
1 tablespoon olive oil
3 garlic cloves, sliced
1 cup thinly sliced red onion (about ½ medium onion)

2 (¼inchthick) lemon slices
1 cup dry white wine
¼ teaspoon kosher or sea salt
¼ teaspoon freshly ground black pepper
Fresh lemon wedges, for garnish

Directions: Rinse the mussels under cold running water, pulling off any beards and discarding any mussels that are open and do not close when tapped. In a large pot or Dutch oven, heat the olive oil over medium heat. Add the garlic and red onion, and cook until the onion is softened, about 5 minutes. Add the lemon slices, white wine, salt, and pepper to the pot. Bring to a boil, then reduce the heat to medium-low. Add the mussels to the pot and stir to coat them in the white wine sauce. Cover and cook until the mussels have opened, about 5-7 minutes. Discard any mussels that do not open. Divide the mussels and white wine sauce among bowls. Garnish with fresh lemon wedges and serve hot.

Nutrition: Calories: 344, total fat: 16.3g, saturated fat: 5.8g, total carbs: 11.5g, fiber: 0g, protein: 36.4g, sugar: 1.1g, sodium: 1270mg, phosphorus: 585mg, potassium: 833mg, cholesterol: 92mg

Mediterranean Trout with Sautéed Vegetables

Prep time: 10 minutes **Cook time:** 20 minutes **Serves** 4

Ingredients:
2 pounds (907 g) rainbow trout fillets
Salt and ground white pepper, to taste
1 tablespoon olive oil
1 pound (454 g) asparagus
4 medium golden potatoes, thinly sliced
1 garlic clove, finely minced
1 scallion, thinly sliced, green and white parts separated
2 Roma tomatoes, chopped
1 large carrot, thinly sliced
8 pitted kalamata olives, chopped
¼ cup ground cumin
2 tablespoons paprika
2 tablespoons dried parsley
1 tablespoon vegetable bouillon seasoning
½ cup dry white wine

Directions: Preheat your oven to 400°F (200°C). Season the trout fillets with salt and white pepper. Heat the olive oil in a large oven-safe skillet over medium heat. Add the trout fillets and cook for 2-3 minutes on each side, or until they are golden brown. Remove the skillet from the heat and transfer the trout fillets to a plate. Set them aside. In the same skillet, add the asparagus, potatoes, garlic, scallion, tomatoes, and carrot. Sauté the vegetables for 5-7 minutes, or until they are tender. Stir in the kalamata olives, cumin, paprika, parsley, and vegetable bouillon seasoning. Place the trout fillets back into the skillet, on top of the vegetables. Pour the white wine over the trout and vegetables. Cover the skillet with aluminum foil and bake in the preheated oven for 15 minutes. Remove the foil and bake for an additional 5 minutes. Garnish with the scallion greens.

Nutrition: Calories: 495, total fat: 19.3g, saturated fat: 5.2g, total carbs: 41.2g, fiber: 7.1g, protein: 40.2g, sugar: 8.1g, sodium: 732mg, cholesterol: 110mg

Superfood Salmon Salad Bowl

Preparation time: 5 minutes **Cooking time**: 10 minutes **Serves**: 2

Ingredients:

Salmon:
2 fillets wild salmon
Salt and black pepper, to taste
2 tsp extra-virgin avocado oil
Dressing:
1 tbsp capers
1 tsp Dijon or wholegrain mustard
1 tbsp apple cider vinegar or fresh lemon juice
3 tbsp extravirgin olive oil
1 tsp coconut aminos
Salt and black pepper, to taste
Salad:
½ medium cucumber, diced
1 cup sugar snap peas, sliced into matchsticks
½ small red bell pepper, sliced
⅓ cup pitted Kalamata olives, halved
2 sundried tomatoes, chopped
1 medium avocado, diced
3 tbsp chopped fresh herbs, such as dill, chives, parsley, and/or basil
1 tbsp pumpkin seeds
1 tbsp sunflower seeds

Directions: Preheat your grill to medium-high heat. Season the salmon fillets with salt and black pepper, and brush with avocado oil. Grill the salmon for about 4 minutes on each side, or until it's cooked to your desired level of doneness. In a small bowl, whisk together the capers, mustard, vinegar or lemon juice, olive oil, coconut aminos, salt, and black pepper. In a large salad bowl, combine the cucumber, sugar snap peas, red bell pepper, olives, sundried tomatoes, avocado, and fresh herbs. Once the salmon has cooled slightly, flake it into large chunks and add it to the salad bowl. Drizzle the dressing over the top of the salad and toss everything together until it's evenly coated. Sprinkle the pumpkin seeds and sunflower seeds over the top of the salad, and serve it immediately.

Nutrition: Calories: 660, fat: 54g, protein: 31g, carbs: 18g, fiber: 9g, sodium: 509mg

Baked Halibut with Eggplants

Servings:4 **Cooking Time:**35 Minutes

Ingredients:
2 tbsp olive oil
¼ cup tomato sauce
4 halibut fillets, boneless
2 eggplants, sliced
Salt and black pepper to taste
2 tbsp balsamic vinegar
2 tbsp chives, chopped

Directions: Preheat your oven to 400°F (200°C). In a bowl, mix together the tomato sauce, 1 tbsp of olive oil, and the balsamic vinegar. Spread a small amount of the tomato sauce mixture on the bottom of an ovenproof dish. Place the halibut fillets on top of the sauce and season them with salt and pepper. Arrange the sliced eggplants around the halibut in the dish. Brush the eggplants with the remaining 1 tbsp of olive oil and season them with salt and pepper. Pour the remaining tomato sauce mixture over the halibut and eggplants. Bake the dish in the preheated oven for 20-25 minutes or until the halibut is cooked through and the eggplants are tender. Garnish with chopped chives.

Nutrition per serving: Calories: 300; Fat: 13g; Protein: 16g; Carbs: 19g.

Grilled Oysters and Tarragon Butter

Prep Time: 15 Minutes **Cooking Time:** 10 Minutes **Additional Time:** 0 Minutes **Total Time:** 25 Minutes **Servings:** 4

Ingredients:
12 large oysters
1/2 cup tarragon leaves
8 oz. butter
1 shallot, diced
1 tbsp. white wine vinegar
1/8 tsp. salt

Directions: Preheat your grill to high heat. In a small saucepan, melt the butter over medium heat. Add the diced shallot and cook until translucent, about 2-3 minutes. Stir in the tarragon leaves and cook for an additional minute. Remove the pan from the heat and stir in the white wine vinegar and salt. Shuck the oysters and place them on the grill, flat side up. Grill for 1-2 minutes, or until the oysters start to bubble and the edges start to curl. Remove the oysters from the grill and top each one with a spoonful of the tarragon butter. Serve immediately.

Nutrition: Calories: 438, Total Fat: 45.6 g, Saturated Fat: 28.5 g, Cholesterol: 171 mg, Sodium: 476 mg, Total Carbohydrates: 3.5 g, Dietary Fiber: 0.4 g, Sugar: 0.4 g, Protein: 8.4 g

Peppercorn-seared Tuna Steaks

Servings: 2 **Cooking Time:** 10 Minutes

Ingredients:
2 ahi tuna steaks
1 teaspoon kosher salt
¼ teaspoon cayenne pepper
2 tablespoons olive oil
1 teaspoon whole peppercorns

Directions: Preheat your grill or stovetop griddle to high heat. In a small bowl, mix together the salt, cayenne pepper, and whole peppercorns. Rub the mixture all over the tuna steaks, making sure to coat both sides evenly. Heat the olive oil in a large skillet over high heat. When the oil is hot, add the tuna steaks and cook for 2-3 minutes on each side, or until they are seared and cooked to your desired level of doneness. Remove the tuna steaks from the skillet and let them rest for a few minutes before slicing and serving. Enjoy your peppercorn-seared tuna steaks with your choice of side dishes. Some delicious options include grilled vegetables, a crisp salad, or a bowl of steaming rice.

Nutrition per serving: Calories: 260; Fat: 14.3g; Protein: 33.4g; Carbs: 0.2g.

Poached Salmon with Mustard Sauce

Prep time: 15 minutes **Cook time:** 20 minutes **Serves** 2

MUSTARD SAUCE:
¼ cup plain Greek yogurt
2 tablespoons Dijon mustard
1½ teaspoons dried tarragon
Pinch salt
Pinch freshly ground black pepper
SALMON:

10 ounces (284 g) salmon fillets
1 tablespoon olive oil
Salt and freshly ground black pepper, to taste
½ fresh lemon, sliced
¼ cup dry white wine
Juice of ½ lemon
¼ cup water

Directions: In a bowl, combine the Greek yogurt, Dijon mustard, tarragon, salt, and pepper. Set aside. Season the salmon fillets with salt and pepper. Heat the olive oil in a large skillet over medium heat. Add the salmon fillets to the skillet and cook for 3-4 minutes on each side, or until they are golden brown and cooked through. While the salmon is cooking, prepare the poaching liquid. In a saucepan, bring the lemon slices, white wine, lemon juice, and water to a boil. Reduce the heat to a gentle simmer and carefully add the cooked salmon fillets to the pan. Poach the salmon for 4-5 minutes, or until it is fully cooked and flakes easily with a fork. Remove the salmon from the poaching liquid and place it on a serving plate. Spoon the mustard sauce over the top of the salmon and serve immediately. **TIP:** You can try other fresh herbs of your choice, such as thyme, oregano or rosemary.

Nutrition: Calories: 330, total fat: 21.2g, total carbs: 3.2g, fiber: 0g, protein: 22.2g, sugar: 2.1g, sodium: 443mg, cholesterol: 70mg

Salmon with Creamy Zucchini

Prep time: 15 min | **Cook time:** 10 min | **Servings:** 2

Ingredients
2 (8 oz.) salmon fillets, skin on
Salt and pepper to taste
1 tsp olive oil
For the zucchini:
2 large zucchinis, trimmed and spiralized
1 avocado, peeled and chopped
A small handful of parsley, chopped
½ garlic clove, minced
A small handful of cherry tomatoes, halved
A small handful of black olives, chopped
2 tbsps. pine nuts, toasted

Directions Preheat your oven to 400°F (200°C). Season the salmon fillets with salt and pepper on both sides. Heat the olive oil in an oven-safe skillet over medium-high heat. Place the salmon fillets in the skillet, skin-side down. Cook for 2-3 minutes, or until the skin is crispy. Flip the fillets and transfer the skillet to the preheated oven. Bake for 8-10 minutes, or until the salmon is cooked through. While the salmon is baking, spiralize the zucchini using a spiralizer or a vegetable peeler. In a separate skillet, heat a small amount of oil over medium heat. Add the spiralized zucchini and sauté for 2-3 minutes, or until tender. Add the avocado, parsley, garlic, cherry tomatoes, black olives, and pine nuts to the skillet with the zucchini. Stir to combine. Cook for an additional 1-2 minutes, or until the vegetables are heated through. Serve the baked salmon with the creamy zucchini mixture on top.

Nutrition: Calories: 726, Fat: 48g, Saturated Fat: 8g, Cholesterol: 123mg, Sodium: 754mg, Carbohydrates: 32g, Fiber: 14g, Sugar: 14g, Protein: 46g

Lime-orange Squid Meal

Servings: 4 **Cooking Time:** 30 Minutes

Ingredients:
1 lb baby squid, cleaned, body and tentacles chopped
3 tbsp olive oil
½ cup green olives, chopped
½ tsp lime zest, grated
1 tbsp lime juice
½ tsp orange zest, grated
1 tsp red pepper flakes
1 tbsp parsley, chopped
4 garlic cloves, minced
1 shallot, chopped
1 cup vegetable stock
2 tbsp red wine vinegar
Salt and black pepper to taste

Directions: Preheat your grill to high heat. In a bowl, mix together the lime zest, lime juice, orange zest, red pepper flakes, parsley, garlic, and shallot. Place the squid in a bowl and pour the olive oil and lime-orange mixture over the top. Toss to coat the squid evenly. Thread the squid onto skewers, leaving a bit of space between each piece. Grill the squid for 2-3 minutes on each side, or until it's cooked to your desired level of doneness. While the squid is grilling, heat the vegetable stock and red wine vinegar in a small saucepan over medium heat. Bring the mixture to a boil, then reduce the heat to low and let it simmer for a few minutes. Once the squid is cooked, transfer it to a plate and pour the hot vegetable stock mixture over the top. Garnish with the chopped olives and serve immediately.

Nutrition per serving: Calories: 310; Fat: 10g; Protein: 12g; Carbs: 23g.

Escarole & White Bean Salad with Swordfish

Preparation Time: 15 minutes **Cooking Time:** 20 minutes **Servings:** 1

Ingredients:
¼ cup extra-virgin olive oil
One teaspoon herb de Provence
12 cups chopped escarole
¼ cup very thinly sliced red onion
Two tablespoons lemon juice
One teaspoon Dijon mustard
½ teaspoon salt, divided
½ teaspoon ground pepper, divided
One 15ounce can of white beans, rinsed
Two 10ounce swordfish steaks

Directions: Preheat your grill to medium-high heat. In a bowl, whisk together the olive oil, herb de Provence, ¼ tsp of the salt, and ¼ tsp of the pepper. Place the swordfish steaks on a plate and brush both sides with the olive oil mixture. Grill the swordfish for about 3-4 minutes on each side, or until it is cooked to your desired doneness. In a larger bowl, combine the escarole, red onion, lemon juice, Dijon mustard, remaining salt and pepper, and white beans. Once the swordfish has finished grilling, cut it into small pieces and add it to the bowl with the escarole and white beans. Toss everything together until well mixed. Serve the salad, garnished with a sprinkle of additional herbs if desired.

Nutrition: calories 1056, fat 52g, carbohydrate 67g, protein 117g

Baked Fish with Pistachio Crust

Preparation time: 12 min **Cooking time:** 18 to 20 min **Servings:** 4

Ingredients:
5 tablespoons extravirgin olive oil, divided
1 pound (454 g) flaky white fish (such as cod, haddock, or halibut), skin removed
½ cup shelled finely chopped pistachios
½ cup ground flaxseed
Zest and juice of 1 lemon, divided
1 teaspoon ground cumin
1 teaspoon ground allspice
½ teaspoon salt
¼ teaspoon freshly ground black pepper

Directions: First, preheat your oven to 400°F (200°C). Next, brush your fish with 1 tablespoon of olive oil and season it with salt and pepper. In a bowl, mix together the pistachios, flaxseed, lemon zest, cumin, allspice, salt, and pepper. Spread this mixture evenly over the top of your fish.
Heat 2 tablespoons of olive oil in a large, ovenproof skillet over medium-high heat. Place the fish in the skillet and cook for 2 minutes on each side, or until it is golden brown. Transfer the skillet to the oven and bake for 10 minutes, or until the fish is cooked through and the pistachio crust is crispy. While the fish is baking, prepare your escarole and white bean salad. In a large bowl, whisk together the remaining 2 tablespoons of olive oil, lemon juice, and Dijon mustard. Add the escarole, red onion, salt, and pepper, and toss to coat. To serve, place a piece of fish on each plate and top it with a generous scoop of escarole and white bean salad.

Nutrition: calories: 510, fat: 42.0g, protein: 27.0g, carbs: 9.0g, fiber: 6.0g, sodium: 331mg

Shrimp with Tomatoes and Feta

Serves: 4 **Readiness: Time:** 20 minutes

Ingredients:
2 tablespoons margarine
1 tablespoon garlic, minced
1 pound shrimp, stripped and deveined
14 ounces canned crushed tomatoes
1 cup feta cheese, crumbled

Directions: Preheat your oven to 400ºF (200ºC). Heat the margarine in a large skillet over medium heat. Add the garlic and cook for 1 minute, stirring frequently, until fragrant. Add the shrimp to the skillet and cook until they are pink and opaque, about 2-3 minutes per side. Add the canned tomatoes to the skillet and stir to combine. Bring the mixture to a simmer and cook for an additional 5 minutes. Remove the skillet from the heat and sprinkle the feta cheese over the top of the shrimp and tomato mixture. Transfer the skillet to the preheated oven and bake for 10-15 minutes, or until the feta cheese is melted and bubbly. Serve hot, garnished with additional chopped fresh herbs if desired.

Nutrition: Calories 218, Total Fat 10.5g, Saturated Fat 6.6g, Cholesterol 192mg, Sodium 618mg, Total Carbohydrate 7.9g, Dietary Fibre 2.2g, Total Sugars 4.7g, Protein 22.5g, Potassium 150mg

Shrimp & Salmon in Tomato Sauce

Servings: 4 **Cooking Time:** 25 Minutes

Ingredients:
1 lb shrimp, peeled and deveined
2 tbsp olive oil
1 lb salmon fillets
Salt and black pepper to taste
1 cups tomatoes, chopped

1 onion, chopped
2 garlic cloves, minced
¼ tsp red pepper flakes
1 cup fish stock
1 tbsp cilantro, chopped

Directions: To begin, heat the olive oil in a large pan over medium heat. Add the shrimp and salmon fillets and season with salt and black pepper. Cook until the seafood is pink and opaque, about 2-3 minutes on each side. Remove the shrimp and salmon from the pan and set aside. In the same pan, add the chopped tomatoes, onion, garlic, and red pepper flakes. Cook until the vegetables are soft and fragrant, about 5 minutes. Pour in the fish stock and bring to a simmer. Add the cooked shrimp and salmon back into the pan and simmer until the sauce has thickened, about 10 minutes. Garnish with chopped cilantro and serve over rice or with a side of your choice.

Nutrition per serving: Calories: 240, Fat: 16g, Protein: 18g, Carbs: 22g.

Spicy Cod Fillets

Servings:4 **Cooking Time:**35 Minutes

Ingredients:
2 tbsp olive oil
1 tsp lime juice
Salt and black pepper to taste
1 tsp sweet paprika
1 tsp chili powder
1 onion, chopped
2 garlic cloves, minced
4 cod fillets, boneless
1 tsp ground coriander
½ cup fish stock
½ lb cherry tomatoes, cubed

Directions: Preheat your oven to 400°F (200°C). In a small bowl, mix together the olive oil, lime juice, paprika, chili powder, and a pinch each of salt and black pepper. Place the cod fillets in a baking dish and brush with the spice mixture. Bake the cod for about 10 minutes, or until it flakes easily with a fork. Meanwhile, heat a pan over medium heat and add the remaining olive oil. Add the onion and garlic and sauté until the onion is translucent. Stir in the ground coriander and cherry tomatoes and cook for an additional 2 minutes. Add the fish stock to the pan and bring to a boil. Reduce the heat and simmer for 5 minutes, or until the sauce has thickened slightly. Serve the cod fillets with the tomato sauce spooned over top and garnished with fresh herbs, if desired.

Nutrition: Calories: 240, Fat: 17g, Protein: 17g, Carbs: 26g.

Salmon with Garlic and Basil Potatoes

Serves: 4 Readiness: Time: 10 minutes

Ingredients:
1 lb. infant potatoes
4 tablespoons margarine, partitioned
4 salmon filets
4 cloves garlic, minced
1 teaspoon dried basil

Directions: Preheat your oven to 400°F (200°C). Wash the baby potatoes and slice them into thin rounds. Melt 2 tablespoons of butter in a large oven-safe pan over medium heat. Add the potatoes to the pan and cook for about 5 minutes, stirring occasionally, until they start to soften. In a small bowl, mix together the minced garlic, dried basil, and the remaining 2 tablespoons of butter. Place the salmon fillets on top of the potatoes in the pan. Spread the garlic and basil butter over the top of the salmon fillets. Place the pan in the oven and bake for about 15-20 minutes, or until the salmon is cooked through and the potatoes are tender. Serve hot, garnished with a sprinkle of fresh chopped parsley and lemon zing if desired.

Nutrition: Calories 408, Total Fat 22.6g, Saturated Fat 8.9g, Cholesterol 109mg, Sodium 172mg, Total Carbohydrate 15.1g, Dietary Fibre 2.9g, Total Sugars 0g, Protein 37.8g, Potassium 1168mg

Fish and Potatoes

Serves: 4 **Time:** quarterhour

Ingredients:
1 lb. cod filets, dig strips.
1 onion, hacked
1 lb. potatoes, dig 3D squares
4 cups vegetable stock
1 teaspoon old inlet preparing

Directions: Preheat your oven to 375°F (190°C). In a large baking dish, place the cod filets in an even layer. Top the cod with the chopped onion, potatoes, and old bay seasoning. Pour the vegetable stock over everything in the baking dish. Cover the dish with aluminum foil and bake for 25 minutes. Remove the foil and bake for an additional 10 minutes or until the fish is cooked through and the potatoes are tender. Serve hot, garnished with chopped fresh herbs if desired.

Nutrition: Calories 278, Total Fat 8.5g, Saturated Fat 1.4g, Cholesterol 50mg, Sodium 981mg, Total Carbohydrate 21.3g, Dietary Fibre 3.3g, Total Sugars 3.2g, Protein 29.1g, Potassium 1144mg

Fish with Pesto Pasta

Serves: 8 **Time:** quarterhour

Ingredients:
16 oz. dry pasta
2 cups pesto sauce
1/2 cup weighty cream
12 oz. cooked salmon, broken into drops

Directions: Bring a large pot of salted water to a boil. Add the pasta and cook according to package instructions. Drain the pasta and return it to the pot. Add the pesto sauce and heavy cream and toss to combine. Divide the pasta among serving bowls and top with the salmon flakes. Serve immediately.

Nutrition: Calories 380, Total Fat 19.7g, Saturated Fat 4.8g, Cholesterol 78mg, Sodium 226mg, Total Carbohydrate 33.2g, Dietary Fibre 0.5g, Total Sugars 2g, Protein 17.8g, Potassium 270mg

Steamed Trout with Lemon Herb Crust

Preparation time: 10 minutes **Cooking time:** 15 minutes **Servings:** 2

Ingredients:
3 tablespoons olive oil
3 garlic cloves, chopped
2 tablespoons fresh lemon juice

1 tablespoon chopped fresh mint
1 tablespoon chopped fresh parsley
¼ teaspoon dried ground thyme
1 teaspoon sea salt
1 pound (454 g) fresh trout (2 pieces)
2 cups fish stock

Directions: In a small bowl, mix together the olive oil, garlic, lemon juice, mint, parsley, thyme, and salt to create the herb crust. Place the trout fillets in a large baking dish, and pour the herb crust mixture over the top of the fillets. Preheat your steamer or a large pot fitted with a steamer basket. Place the baking dish with the trout in the steamer basket, and pour the fish stock into the pot. Cover and steam the trout for 10-15 minutes, or until the fish is cooked through and flakes easily with a fork. Serve the steamed trout with the lemon herb crust, alongside your choice of sides and garnishes.

Nutrition: calories 477, fat 29.6g, protein 51.7g, carbs 3.6g, fiber 0.2g, sodium 2011mg

Air fryer Panko-crusted Fish Nuggets

Servings: 4 **Cooking Time:** 10 Mints
Ingredients:
2 cups fish fillets (skinless, cut into cubes)
1 egg, beaten
5 tablespoons flour
5 tablespoons water
Kosher salt and pepper, to taste
¼ cup whole wheat breadcrumbs
1 tablespoon smoked paprika
1 tablespoon garlic powder

Directions: Preheat your air fryer to 375°F (190°C). In a shallow dish, mix together the flour, water, salt, and pepper. Dip each fish cube into the flour mixture, making sure to coat it evenly. In a separate shallow dish, mix together the breadcrumbs, paprika, and garlic powder. Dip each floured fish cube into the breadcrumb mixture, coating it evenly. Place the breaded fish cubes in the air fryer basket, making sure not to overcrowd it. Spray the fish with cooking spray. Cook the fish for 8-10 minutes, until it is crispy and golden brown. Serve immediately, with your choice of dipping sauce.

Nutrition: calories 184.2, Protein: 19g, Total Fat: 3.3g, Net Carb: 10g

Crab Cakes

Servings: 6 **Cooking Time:** 10 Mints
Ingredients:
4 cups of crab meat
2 eggs
¼ cup of whole wheat bread crumbs
2 tablespoons of mayonnaise
1 teaspoon of Worcestershire sauce
1 and ½ teaspoons of Old Bay seasoning
1 teaspoon of Dijon mustard
Freshly ground black pepper, to taste
¼ cup of green onion, chopped

Directions: In a large bowl, mix together the crab meat, eggs, bread crumbs, mayonnaise, Worcestershire sauce, Old Bay seasoning, Dijon mustard, and black pepper. Using your hands or a spoon, shape the mixture into small patties about the size of your palm. Heat a large pan over medium heat and add a little bit of oil. Once the pan is hot, add the crab cakes and cook for about 3-4 minutes on each side, until they are golden brown. Garnish with chopped green onion.

Nutrition: calories 218 Fat: 13 g Net Carbs: 5.6 g Protein: 16.7g

Grilled Fish with Salad

Prep time: 8 minutes **Cook time:** 10 minutes **Serving:** 2

Ingredients:
1 pound of fish (your choice)
1 tomato
1 lemon
Ground black pepper, to taste
1 tablespoon extra virgin olive oil
5 basil leaves
2 tablespoons parsley leaves

Directions: Preheat your grill to medium-high heat. Cut the fish into desired size pieces and season with ground black pepper. Slice the tomato and set aside. Zest and juice the lemon, reserving both. In a small bowl, mix together the lemon zest, lemon juice, olive oil, and a pinch of salt. Place the fish on the grill and brush with the lemon mixture. Grill for about 4-5 minutes on each side, or until the fish is cooked through. In a separate bowl, combine the sliced tomato, chopped basil and parsley, and a pinch of salt. Serve the grilled fish with the tomato salad on the side.

Nutrition per serving: Calories: 300, Fat: 14g, Saturated Fat: 2g, Cholesterol: 75mg, Sodium: 180mg, Carbohydrates: 16g, Fiber: 4g, Sugar: 7g, Protein: 32g

VEGETARIAN RECIPES

Vegetarian Pumpkin Soup Mediterranean Style

Total Time 30 minutes **Difficulty Level** low **Servings** 6

Ingredients:
1 can of pumpkin puree (15 ounces)
1 cup of mushrooms
1 cup of light cream
2 teaspoons of hot sauce
3 vegetarian sausage links
1 quart of vegetable broth
1/2 minced onion
1/4 cup of Parmesan cheese grated
1 clove of garlic
1 tablespoon of Italian seasoning

Directions: In a pot, heat 1 tablespoon of olive oil over medium heat. Add the minced onion and garlic, and cook until the onion is translucent. Add the sliced mushrooms and cook for an additional 2-3 minutes. Pour in the vegetable broth and bring the mixture to a boil. Add the can of pumpkin puree, hot sauce, and Italian seasoning. Stir to combine. Reduce the heat to low and simmer for 15-20 minutes. Stir in the light cream and sliced vegetarian sausage. Garnish with grated Parmesan cheese.

Nutrition: Calories: 150, Fat: 10g, Cholesterol: 20mg, Sodium: 940mg, Carbohydrates: 14g, Fiber: 3g, Sugar: 6g, Protein: 7g.

Balsamic Brussels sprouts

Preparation Time: 10 minutes **Cooking Time:** 40 minutes **Servings:** 6

Ingredients:
2 tablespoons brown sugar
½ cup balsamic vinegar
2 lb. Brussels sprouts, trimmed and sliced in half 2 tablespoons olive oil
2 tablespoons butter, cut into cubes
Salt and pepper to taste
¼ cup Parmesan cheese, grated

Directions: Preheat your oven to 425°F (220°C). In a saucepan over medium heat, combine the brown sugar and balsamic vinegar. Bring to a boil, then reduce the heat to low and let it simmer for about 5 minutes, or until it has reduced by about half and is thick and syrupy. While the balsamic reduction is cooking, place the Brussels sprouts in a bowl. Add the olive oil and toss until the sprouts are evenly coated. Spread the sprouts out onto a baking sheet, making sure they are in a single layer. Sprinkle with salt and pepper. Place the baking sheet in the preheated oven and roast for 20-25 minutes, or until the sprouts are tender. Remove the baking sheet from the oven and sprinkle the butter cubes over the top of the sprouts. Return the baking sheet to the oven and roast for an additional 5 minutes, or until the butter has melted. Drizzle the balsamic reduction over the top of the sprouts and sprinkle with Parmesan cheese. Return the baking sheet to the oven and roast for an additional 5 minutes. Garnished the hot Brussels sprouts with additional Parmesan cheese if desired.

Nutrition: Calories 193, Fat 10 g, Cholesterol 13.2 mg, Carbohydrates 21.9 g, Fiber 6.2 g, Protein 6.9 g, Sugars 11.1 g

Mediterranean Zucchini & Eggplant

Preparation Time: 15 minutes **Cooking Time:** 3 hours **Servings:** 4

Ingredients:
1 tablespoon olive oil
1 onion, diced
4 cloves garlic, minced
1 red bell pepper, chopped
4 tomatoes, diced
1 zucchini, chopped
1 lb. eggplant, sliced into cubes
Salt and pepper to taste
2 teaspoons dried basil
4 oz. feta cheese

Directions: Heat the olive oil in a pan over medium heat. Add the onion and garlic and cook for about 5 minutes, or until the onion is translucent. Add the red bell pepper, tomatoes, zucchini, and eggplant to the pan. Season with salt, pepper, and basil. Cook for about 10 minutes, or until the vegetables are tender. Sprinkle the feta cheese over the top of the vegetables. Cover the pan and cook for an additional 2-3 minutes, or until the cheese is melted. Garnish with additional fresh basil if desired.

Nutrition: Calories 341, Fat 12 g, Cholesterol 25 mg, Carbohydrate 51 g, Fiber 11 g, Protein 13 g, Sugars 13 g

Roasted Baby Carrots

Preparation Time: 5 minutes **Cooking Time:** 25-30 minutes **Servings:** 6

Ingredients:
1 pound baby carrots, washed and trimmed
2 tablespoons olive oil
2 teaspoons dried thyme
1 teaspoon garlic powder
1/2 teaspoon salt

1/4 teaspoon black pepper

Directions: Preheat your oven to 400°F (200°C). In a bowl, whisk together the olive oil, thyme, garlic powder, salt, and pepper. Next, place the carrots in a single layer on a baking sheet lined with parchment paper. Drizzle the oil mixture over the carrots, using a brush or your hands to evenly coat them. Roast the carrots in the preheated oven for 25-30 minutes, or until they are tender and slightly caramelized. Halfway through cooking, give the carrots a toss to ensure even cooking. Remove the carrots from the oven. Garnish with a sprinkle of salt and serve hot.

Nutrition per serving: Calories: 80, Fat: 7g, Sodium: 220mg, Carbohydrates: 6g, Fiber: 2g, Sugar: 4g, Protein: 1g

Stuffed Pepper Stew

Preparation time: 20 minutes **Cooking time:** 40 minutes **Serves** 2

Ingredients:
1 tablespoon olive oil
1 onion, diced
2 cloves garlic, minced
2 bell peppers, halved and seeded
1 cup quinoa, rinsed
2 cups vegetable broth
1 can diced tomatoes
1 teaspoon dried basil
Salt and pepper, to taste
1/2 cup shredded mozzarella cheese

Directions: Preheat your oven to 350°F (180°C). In a saucepan, heat the olive oil over medium heat. Add the onion and garlic and cook until the onion is translucent, about 5 minutes. Add the quinoa, vegetable broth, diced tomatoes, and basil to the saucepan. Bring to a boil, then reduce the heat to low and simmer for 20 minutes, or until the quinoa is cooked. Meanwhile, place the bell peppers in a baking dish. Fill each pepper half with the quinoa mixture, then top with the mozzarella cheese. Bake for 20 minutes, or until the peppers are tender and the cheese is melted and bubbly. Serve hot.

Nutrition per serving: Calories: 250, Fat: 12g, Protein: 15g, Carbohydrates: 25g

Easy vegetarian pizzas

Preparation Time: 20 minutes **Cooking Time:** 15 minutes **Servings:** 2

Ingredients:
2 small pre-made pizza crusts
1 cup tomato sauce
1 cup shredded mozzarella cheese
1 cup chopped vegetables (such as bell peppers, onions, mushrooms, and olives)
2 tablespoons chopped fresh herbs (such as basil and oregano)

Directions: Preheat your oven to 400°F (200°C). Place the pizza crusts on a baking sheet. Spread the tomato sauce over the crusts, leaving a border around the edges. Sprinkle the cheese over the sauce. Top with chopped vegetables and fresh herbs. Bake for 10-15 minutes, or until the cheese is melted and the crust is golden brown. Let cool outside of the oven for a few minutes before slicing.

Nutrition per serving: Calories: 400, Fat: 15g, Protein: 15g, Carbohydrates: 50g, Fiber: 4g, Sodium: 800mg

Vegetable and tofu nasi goreng

Preparation Time: 15 minutes **Cooking Time:** 15 minutes **Servings:** 4

Ingredients:
1/2 head of cauliflower, chopped

400g broccoli, chopped
2 large carrots, chopped
300g block of firm tofu
1 1/2 tablespoons peanut oil
4 green onions, sliced, plus extra for serving
5cm piece of fresh ginger, finely grated
1/4 cup vegetarian oyster sauce
1 tablespoon kecap manis
1 cup bean sprouts, trimmed
4 eggs
1 cup fresh coriander leaves, plus extra for serving
1 tablespoon sambal oelek
Lime wedges, for serving

Directions: Heat a large wok or frying pan over medium-high heat. Add the peanut oil and heat until hot. Add the tofu to the wok and stir-fry for 2-3 minutes until browned. Remove from the wok and set aside. In the same wok, add the cauliflower, broccoli, and carrots. Stir-fry for 3-4 minutes until the vegetables are tender. Add the green onions and ginger to the wok and stir-fry for another minute. Stir in the vegetarian oyster sauce and kecap manis, then add the bean sprouts and stir-fry for another minute. Push the vegetables to the side of the wok and crack the eggs into the center. Scramble the eggs until cooked, then mix them into the vegetables. Add the reserved tofu back into the wok and stir to combine. Stir in the fresh coriander leaves and sambal oelek. Serve the nasi goreng hot, garnished with extra sliced green onions and coriander leaves, and accompanied by lime wedges.

Nutrition: Calories: 345, Protein: 20g, Fat: 20g, Carbohydrates: 27g, Fiber: 8g, Sugar: 12g

Portobello caprese

Prep time: 15 minutes **Cook time:** 30 minutes **Serves** 2

Ingredients:
1 tablespoon olive oil, plus more for greasing the baking pan
1 cup cherry tomatoes
Salt and freshly ground black pepper, to taste
4 large fresh basil leaves, thinly sliced, divided
3 medium garlic cloves, minced
2 large portobello mushrooms, stems removed
4 pieces mini Mozzarella balls (Ciliegine), halved
1 tablespoon Parmesan cheese, grated

Directions: To start, preheat your oven to 400°F (200°C) and lightly grease a baking pan with olive oil. Next, in a small bowl, mix together the cherry tomatoes, a pinch of salt, a pinch of black pepper, and 2 of the sliced basil leaves. Set aside. In a separate small bowl, mix together the minced garlic, 1 tablespoon of olive oil, and a pinch of salt. Brush this mixture over the portobello mushrooms and place them on the prepared baking pan. Bake the mushrooms for 15-20 minutes, or until they are tender and juicy. While the mushrooms are baking, place the mini Mozzarella balls in a separate small bowl and toss them with the remaining 2 sliced basil leaves. When the mushrooms are finished cooking, top each one with half of the cherry tomato mixture, 4 halved mini Mozzarella balls, and a sprinkle of grated Parmesan cheese. Return the mushrooms to the oven and bake for an additional 5-10 minutes, or until the cheese is melted and bubbly. Serve the Portobello caprese immediately, garnished with a sprinkle of fresh basil and a squeeze of lemon juice, if desired.

Nutrition: calories: 285, total fat: 21.8g, cholesterol: 42mg, total carbs: 11.2g, fiber: 2.1g, sugars: 5.2g, protein: 14.3g, sodium: 354mg

Vegetarian Bourguignon

Total Time 60 minutes **Difficulty Level** low **Servings** 4

Ingredients:
2 tablespoons olive oil, divided
1 pint brown champignon mushrooms
1 yellow onion, sliced
1 large garlic clove
1 large carrot
2 thyme leaves, stripped from stem
1 eggplant
1 sprig fresh rosemary
Salt and black pepper, to taste
1/2 cup hearty red wine
2 Roma tomatoes, chopped
1/2 cup vegetable broth
2 tablespoons tomato paste

Directions: Heat 1 tablespoon of olive oil in a large, heavy-bottomed pot over medium heat. Add the mushrooms and cook for 5 minutes, stirring occasionally, until they start to release their liquid. Add the onion, garlic, carrot, thyme, and eggplant to the pot. Cook for 5 more minutes, stirring occasionally, until the vegetables are softened. Add the rosemary, salt, black pepper, red wine, tomatoes, vegetable broth, and tomato paste to the pot. Bring to a boil, then reduce the heat to low and simmer for 30 minutes. Meanwhile, heat the remaining 1 tablespoon of olive oil in a large skillet over medium heat. Add the cooked vegetables to the skillet and cook for 5 minutes, stirring occasionally, until they start to brown. Serve the Vegetarian Bourguignon hot, garnished with fresh herbs and a sprinkle of grated Parmesan cheese, if desired.

Nutrition per serving: Calories: 163 Fat: 8.6g Saturated fat: 1.1g Unsaturated fat: 7.5g Trans fat: 0g Carbohydrates: 19g Sugar: 8g Fiber: 5g Protein: 6g Sodium: 649mg Cholesterol: 0mg

Brussels Sprouts With Balsamic Glaze

Prep time: 15 minutes **Cook time:** 20 minutes **Serves** 6

BALSAMIC GLAZE:
1 cup balsamic vinegar
¼ cup honey
2 tablespoons extravirgin olive oil
2 pounds (907 g) Brussels sprouts, trimmed and halved
2 cups lowsodium vegetable soup
1 teaspoon sea salt
Freshly ground black pepper, to taste
¼ cup Parmesan cheese, grated
¼ cup pine nuts, toasted

Directions: In a small saucepan, combine the balsamic vinegar and honey over medium heat. Bring to a boil, then reduce heat to low and simmer for 10-15 minutes, or until the mixture has reduced and thickened to a glaze consistency. Remove from heat and set aside. Preheat your oven to 400°F (200°C). In a large mixing bowl, toss the Brussels sprouts with the olive oil, salt, and pepper. Spread them out in a single layer on a baking sheet. Roast the Brussels sprouts in the oven for 10-15 minutes, or until they are tender and starting to brown. In the meantime, heat the vegetable soup in a small saucepan over medium heat. When the Brussels sprouts are done, remove them from the oven and transfer them to a serving dish. Pour the hot vegetable soup over the top, then drizzle with the balsamic glaze. Sprinkle with Parmesan cheese and toasted pine nuts.

Nutrition: calories: 270, fat: 10.6g, saturated fat: 1.8g, cholesterol: 4mg, carbs: 38.6g, fiber: 6.9g, sugars: 22.7g, protein: 8.7g, sodium: 700mg

Vegetarian Breakfast Casserole

Preparation Time: 10 minutes **Cooking Time:** 15 minutes **Servings:** 1

Ingredients:
2 medium sweet potatoes peeled and diced
1 red bell pepper diced
1 small head of broccoli
8 ounces whole cremini baby Bella mushrooms
1 teaspoon kosher salt
1 red or yellow onion
½ teaspoon black pepper
3 tablespoons extra virgin olive oil
12 large eggs
½ cup milk
1 garlic clove minced
1 ½ teaspoon Italian seasoning
4 ounces partskim ricotta cheese
Chopped fresh basil

Directions: Preheat your oven to 350°F (180°C). Grease a large baking dish with cooking spray. In a large bowl, toss together the diced sweet potatoes, bell pepper, broccoli, and mushrooms. Season with salt and pepper. Heat the olive oil in a large skillet over medium heat. Add the onion and garlic, and cook until the onion is translucent, about 5 minutes. Add the vegetable mixture to the skillet and cook until the vegetables are tender, about 10 minutes. In a separate bowl, whisk together the eggs, milk, Italian seasoning, and a pinch of salt. Spread the cooked vegetables evenly in the prepared baking dish. Pour the egg mixture over the top. Drop spoonfuls of the ricotta cheese over the top. Bake the casserole for 35-40 minutes, or until the eggs are set and the top is golden brown. Garnish with chopped fresh basil before serving.

Nutrition: Calories: 602 Fat: 41.5g Saturated fat: 13.6g Unsaturated fat: 27.9g Trans fat: 0g Carbohydrates: 43.3g Sugar: 12.1g Fiber: 8.3g Protein: 25.3g Sodium: 1479mg Cholesterol: 506mg

Citrus Pistachios and Asparagus

Prep time: 10 minutes **Cook time:** 10 minutes **Serves** 4

Ingredients:
Zest and juice of 2 clementines or 1 orange
Zest and juice of 1 lemon
1 tablespoon red wine vinegar
3 tablespoons extravirgin olive oil, divided
1 teaspoon salt, divided
¼ teaspoon freshly ground black pepper
½ cup pistachios, shelled
1 pound (454 g) fresh asparagus, trimmed
1 tablespoon water

Directions: To begin, whisk together the clementine or orange zest and juice, lemon zest and juice, red wine vinegar, 2 tablespoons of olive oil, and ½ teaspoon of salt in a small bowl. Next, heat a large skillet over medium-high heat and add the remaining 1 tablespoon of olive oil. Add the pistachios to the skillet and cook, stirring frequently, until they are lightly toasted and fragrant, about 2-3 minutes. Remove the pistachios from the skillet and set aside. Add the asparagus to the skillet and cook for 3-4 minutes, until it is crisp-tender. Stir in the water and the remaining ½ teaspoon of salt, and cook for an additional minute. Finally, drizzle the citrus dressing over the asparagus and sprinkle the toasted pistachios on top. Serve hot.

Nutrition: calories: 211, fat: 17.5g, carbs: 11.2g, fiber: 3.8g, carbs: 7.4g, protein: 5.9g, sodium: 596mg

Vegetarian Barley Risotto

Prep Time: 20 minutes **Cooking Time:** 45 Minutes **Total Time:** 65 Minutes **Servings:** 6

Ingredients:
1 1/2 cups barley
1 broccoli head, sliced into florets
1 zucchini, shredded
1/2 onion, diced
1 yellow squash, grated
2 carrots, shredded
Bay leaf, as per taste
2 garlic cloves, chopped
2 tbsp. extra virgin olive oil
4 1/2 cups vegetable stock
1/2 cup water
Kosher salt and black pepper to taste

Directions: Start by heating 1 tablespoon of the olive oil in a pot over medium heat. Add the onion and garlic and cook until the onion is translucent, about 5 minutes. Next, add the barley to the pot and stir to coat it in the oil and onion mixture. Add the vegetable stock, water, and bay leaf to the pot and bring the mixture to a boil. Reduce the heat to low, cover the pot, and simmer for 45 minutes. While the barley is cooking, heat the remaining 1 tablespoon of olive oil in a separate pan over medium heat. Add the broccoli, zucchini, squash, and carrots to the pan and cook until they are tender, about 10 minutes. When the barley is finished cooking, remove the bay leaf and stir in the cooked vegetables. Season the risotto with salt and pepper to taste. Serve the Vegetarian Barley Risotto hot, garnished with your choice of herbs or cheese.

Nutrition per serving: Calories: 195 Fat: 5.4g Saturated fat: 0.8g Unsaturated fat: 4.6g Trans fat: 0g Carbohydrates: 34.1g Sugar: 4.7g Fiber: 7.4g Protein: 6.4g Sodium: 645mg Cholesterol: 0mg

Vegetarian Spanish Rice

Prep Time: 10 Minutes **Cooking Time:** 25 Minutes **Total Time:** 35 Minutes **Servings:** 4

Ingredients:
1 1/2 cups long grain rice (instant cooking is fine)
14 1/2 oz can of stewed tomatoes
14 1/2 oz can of vegetable broth
1 tsp extra virgin olive oil
1 tsp chili powder
1/4 tsp garlic salt
1/4 tsp dried oregano

Directions: To start, heat the olive oil in a large pan over medium heat. Add the rice and cook, stirring occasionally, until it starts to turn golden brown. Next, add the stewed tomatoes, vegetable broth, chili powder, garlic salt, and oregano to the pan. Bring the mixture to a boil, then reduce the heat to low and simmer for about 20 minutes, or until the rice is tender and the liquid has been absorbed. Serve the vegetarian Spanish rice hot, garnished with a sprinkle of fresh herbs if desired.

Nutrition per serving: Calories: 191 Fat: 1.6g Saturated fat: 0.2g Unsaturated fat: 1.4g Trans fat: 0g Carbohydrates: 41.5g Sugar: 5.5g Fiber: 2.5g Protein: 5.3g Sodium: 523mg Cholesterol: 0mg

Greek Vegetarian Phyllo Pastry Pizza

Prep Time: 20 minutes **Cooking Time:** 20 minutes **Total Time:** 50 minutes **Servings:** 4-6

Ingredients:
10 sheets of phyllo pastry
1/2 cup butter, melted
1 1/2 cups mozzarella cheese, shredded

2/3 cup Parmesan cheese, grated
1 1/2 cups crumbled feta cheese
2/3 cup baby spinach, finely chopped
1 onion, thinly sliced
4 Roma tomatoes, diced lengthwise
2 cups black olives, chopped
2 tsp. dry oregano
1 package of basil, roughly chopped

Directions: Preheat your oven to 350°F (180°C). Lightly brush a baking sheet with melted butter. Lay out 1 sheet of phyllo pastry on the baking sheet and brush with melted butter. Repeat this process with the remaining sheets of phyllo pastry, making sure to brush each sheet with butter before layering it on top of the previous one. In a large mixing bowl, combine the mozzarella cheese, Parmesan cheese, and feta cheese. Sprinkle this mixture over the top of the phyllo pastry. Scatter the baby spinach, onion, tomatoes, and black olives over the cheese mixture. Sprinkle with dry oregano and basil. Bake the pizza in the preheated oven for 20 minutes, or until the phyllo pastry is golden brown and the cheese is melted and bubbly. Serve with additional basil if desired.

Nutrition per serving: Calories: 603 Fat: 41.5g Saturated fat: 22.3g Unsaturated fat: 19.2g Trans fat: 0.5g Carbohydrates: 41.5g Sugar: 5.8g Fiber: 5.5g Protein: 24.8g Sodium: 1196mg Cholesterol: 89mg

Vegetarian Egg Casserole

Prep Time: 15 minutes **Cooking Time:** 35-40 minutes **Total Time:** 45 minutes **Servings:** 6
Ingredients:
7-8 organic eggs
3 oz. chopped mushrooms (optional)
4 oz. canned artichoke hearts, quartered
2 oz. Kalamata olives, diced and pitted
1 tomato, diced
2 shallots, finely sliced
1 bell pepper, chopped into rounds
2 1/2 oz. crumbled feta cheese
1 1/2 cups milk
3 pieces of wholewheat bread (toast), sliced thinly 11/2 tsp. baking powder
Extra virgin olive oil
1/4 tsp. nutmeg
1 1/2 tsp. sweet paprika
Kosher salt and black pepper to taste
1 tsp. dried oregano
1 oz. diced parsley

Directions: Start by preheating your oven to 350°F (180°C). Begin by heating a small amount of olive oil in a skillet over medium heat. Add the mushrooms (if using) and sauté until they are tender and browned. Meanwhile, in a large mixing bowl, whisk together the eggs, milk, baking powder, nutmeg, paprika, salt, pepper, and oregano. Stir in the chopped artichoke hearts, olives, tomato, shallots, bell pepper, feta cheese, and parsley. Grease a 9x13 inch baking dish with olive oil or cooking spray. Arrange the toast slices in the bottom of the dish, then pour the egg mixture over the top. Sprinkle with a little extra feta cheese if desired. Bake the casserole in the preheated oven for 35-40 minutes, or until it is set and the top is golden brown. Let the casserole cool for a few minutes before serving.

Nutrition per serving: Calories: 216 Fat: 14g Saturated fat: 5.5g Unsaturated fat: 8.5g Trans fat: 0g Carbohydrates: 15g Sugar: 6.3g Fiber: 2.4g Protein: 12g Sodium: 466mg Cholesterol: 191mg

SALADS

Greek Style Salad Dip

Total Time: 10 minutes **Difficulty Level:** low **Servings:** 8

Ingredients:
One seeded and chopped tomato
Three finely chopped green onions
1/2 cup of Caesar salad dressing
8 ounces of feta cheese crumbled
1 (2.25 ounces) can of black olives chopped

Directions: In a bowl, combine the tomato, green onions, Caesar dressing, feta cheese, and black olives. Mix until everything is well combined and the ingredients are evenly distributed. Transfer the dip to a serving dish and serve with your choice of crackers, pita chips, or veggies for dipping.

Nutrition per serving: Calories: 107 Fat: 8.6g Saturated fat: 3.9g Unsaturated fat: 4.7g Trans fat: 0g Carbohydrates: 5.5g Sugar: 3.5g Fiber: 1.2g Protein: 3.8g Sodium: 569mg Cholesterol: 18mg

Avocado, Black Bean, and Quinoa Salad

Total Time 30 minutes **Difficulty Level** low **Servings** 4

Ingredients:
1 cup grape tomatoes
2 ½ cups precooked quinoa
1 can of black beans (10 ounces)
½ chopped avocado
1 tablespoons extravirgin olive oil
¼ cup lime juice
½ teaspoon lime zest
1 cup cilantro leaves
½ teaspoon ground black pepper
¼ teaspoon salt
1 clove garlic

Directions: Begin by prepping your ingredients. Halve and chop your grape tomatoes and set them aside. If you don't have precooked quinoa on hand, now is the time to cook it according to the package instructions. Next, drain and rinse your can of black beans, and chop your avocado into small pieces. In a large mixing bowl, combine the quinoa, black beans, and avocado. In a separate small bowl, whisk together the olive oil, lime juice, lime zest, and minced garlic. Pour this dressing over the quinoa mixture and toss to coat. Finally, add in the chopped grape tomatoes, cilantro leaves, ground black pepper, and salt. Toss everything together until well combined, and serve immediately. This Avocado, Black Bean, and Quinoa Salad is best served cold or at room temperature.

Nutrition per serving: Calories: 309 Fat: 13.1g Saturated fat: 2.1g Unsaturated fat: 11g Trans fat: 0g Carbohydrates: 40.6g Sugar: 2.9g Fiber: 8.1g Protein: 10.4g Sodium: 354mg Cholesterol: 0mg

Vegetarian Pasta Salad

Prep Time: 15 minutes **Cooking Time:** 15 minutes **Total Time:** 30 minutes **Servings:** 4

Ingredients:
1 lb. of penne pasta
Dressing:
8 oz. pack of mozzarella cheese, cubed
2 garlic cloves, diced
5 tomatoes, chopped

15 oz. canned artichoke, cubed
4 tsp. balsamic vinegar
3 tsp. maple syrup
2 tsp. Dijon mustard
4 tsp. olive oil
Sea salt and black pepper
1/2 clump of basil, chopped
4 cups arugula

Directions: Start by cooking your penne pasta according to the package instructions, then set it aside to cool. In the meantime, prepare the dressing by whisking together mozzarella cheese, garlic, balsamic vinegar, maple syrup, Dijon mustard, and olive oil. Season with a pinch of sea salt and black pepper. Next, combine the cooled pasta with the chopped tomatoes, artichoke, and arugula in a large mixing bowl. Pour the dressing over the pasta mixture and toss until everything is well coated. Top with a sprinkle of chopped basil and serve chilled or at room temperature.

Nutrition per serving: Calories: 447 Fat: 17.5g Saturated fat: 6.1g Unsaturated fat: 11.4g Trans fat: 0g Carbohydrates: 59.3g Sugar: 13.3g Fiber: 4.8g Protein: 17.3g Sodium: 468mg Cholesterol: 33mg

Italian Tuna and Olive Salad

Prep Time: 5 minutes **Cooking time**: 0 minutes **Serves** 4

Ingredients:
¼ cup olive oil
3 tbsp white wine vinegar
1 tsp salt
1 cup pitted green olives
1 medium red bell pepper, seeded and diced
1 small clove of garlic, minced
2 (6ounce / 170g) cans or jars of tuna in olive oil, well drained
Several leaves of curly green or red lettuce

Directions: Start by whisking together the olive oil, white wine vinegar, and salt in a small bowl. Set aside. In a separate large bowl, combine the green olives, red bell pepper, and minced garlic. Add the drained tuna to the bowl and mix everything together. Pour the dressing over the tuna and vegetable mixture, and toss to coat everything evenly. Arrange several leaves of lettuce on a plate and spoon the tuna salad mixture onto the lettuce. Serve immediately, garnished with additional olives or diced bell pepper if desired.

Nutrition: Calories: 339, fat: 24g, protein: 25g, carbs: 4g, fiber: 2g, sodium: 626mg

Greek Salad with Lemon Oregano Vinaigrette

Preparation time: 15 minutes **Cooking time:** 15 minutes **Serves** 8

Ingredients:
½ red onion, thinly sliced
¼ cup extravirgin olive oil
3 tbsp fresh lemon juice or red wine vinegar
1 clove garlic, minced
1 tsp chopped fresh oregano or ½ tsp dried
½ tsp ground black pepper
¼ tsp kosher salt
4 tomatoes, cut into large chunks
1 large English cucumber, peeled, seeded (if desired), and diced
1 large yellow or red bell pepper, chopped
½ cup pitted kalamata or Niçoise olives, halved
¼ cup chopped fresh flatleaf parsley

4 ounces (113 g) Halloumi or feta cheese, cut into ½' cubes

Directions: In a bowl, whisk together the olive oil, lemon juice or vinegar, garlic, oregano, pepper, and salt. In a larger bowl, combine the tomatoes, cucumber, bell pepper, olives, parsley, and cheese. Add the vinaigrette and toss to coat the vegetables. Let the salad sit for at least 10 minutes to allow the flavors to meld together. Serve chilled or at room temperature, garnished with additional parsley.

Nutrition: Calories: 190, fat: 16g, protein: 5g, carbs: 8g, fiber: 2g, sodium: 554mg

Hazelnuts, Blueberries with Grain Salad

Total Time 20 minutes **Difficulty Level** low **Servings** 4

Ingredients:
1 cup Dry golden quinoa,
1 cup Steelcut oats
2 cups Hazelnuts, roughly chopped
½ cup Dry millet
½ Fresh ginger, half" piece, 1
3 tablespoons Olive oil
1 teaspoon Lemon's zest
1 cup Greek yogurt,
½ cup Maple syrup
¼ teaspoon Nutmeg
2 cups Blueberries

Directions: Start by cooking the quinoa, oats, millet, and ginger in a pot with 4 cups of water. Bring the mixture to a boil, then reduce the heat to a simmer and cook for about 20-25 minutes, or until the grains are tender. In the meantime, preheat your oven to 350°F (180°C). Spread the chopped hazelnuts on a baking sheet and roast for about 10-15 minutes, or until they're fragrant and lightly toasted. Once the grains are cooked, drain off any excess water and transfer them to a large mixing bowl. Stir in the olive oil, lemon zest, and 1/4 teaspoon of nutmeg. In a separate bowl, whisk together the Greek yogurt and maple syrup. Stir the blueberries into the grain mixture, then top with the toasted hazelnuts. Serve the grain salad with a dollop of the maple yogurt on top.

Nutrition per serving: Calories: 649 Fat: 35g Saturated fat: 5.5g Unsaturated fat: 29.5g Trans fat: 0g Carbohydrates: 74g Sugar: 34g Fiber: 8g Protein: 20g Sodium: 84mg Cholesterol: 6mg

Egg Salad Avocado Toast

Total Time 10 minutes **Difficulty Level** low **Servings** 1

Ingredients:
1 hardboiled egg, sliced
1/4 avocado, mashed
1 tablespoon celery, finely diced
1 piece of whole wheat toast
1/2 teaspoon lemon juice
Pinch of salt
1/2 teaspoon hot sauce (optional)

Directions: Start by preparing your hardboiled egg. Place the egg in a small saucepan and cover it with cold water. Bring the water to a boil, then turn off the heat and let the egg sit in the hot water for about 10-12 minutes. Drain the hot water and run the egg under cold water to stop the cooking process. Once cooled, peel the egg and slice it into thin rounds. In a small bowl, mash the avocado with a fork until it is smooth. Spread the mashed avocado onto the piece of toast. Top the avocado with the sliced egg, diced celery, and a sprinkle of lemon juice and salt. If desired, add a drizzle of hot sauce for a little extra kick. Serve immediately.

Nutrition per serving: Calories: 261 Fat: 17.7g Saturated fat: 3.3g Unsaturated fat: 14.4g Trans fat: 0g Carbohydrates: 21.3g Sugar: 2.3g Fiber: 7.6g Protein: 9.6g Sodium: 343mg Cholesterol: 186mg

Spinach Salad Dressing

Preparation Time: 11 minutes **Cooking Time:** 20 minutes **Servings:** 1

Ingredients:
½ cup olive oil
2 tablespoons Worcestershire sauce
¼ cup ketchup
½ cup white sugar
¼ cup red wine vinegar

Directions: In a food processor, combine the olive oil, Worcestershire sauce, ketchup, sugar, and red wine vinegar. Blend until smooth. Pour the dressing over your favorite spinach salad and toss to coat. Serve immediately. This creamy and flavorful dressing is perfect for a classic spinach salad, but it can also be used as a marinade for grilled vegetables or a dipping sauce for crunchy veggies.
Nutrition: Calories: 722, Fat: 77g, Saturated fat: 10g, Cholesterol: 0mg, Sodium: 617mg, Carbohydrates: 39g, Fiber: 1g, Sugar: 36g, Protein: 1g

Mediterranean Inspired Chickpea Salad

Preparation Time: 9 minutes **Cooking Time:** 15 minutes **Servings:** 1

Ingredients:
¼ cup olive oil
1 tablespoon dried oregano
¼ cup red wine vinegar
1 tablespoon chopped garlic
1 (6 ounces) can small black olives, drained
1 (15 ounces) can chickpeas, drained
1 (6 ounces) jar marinated artichoke hearts, drained
1 ½ ounces nonperil capers, rinsed and drained
3 ounces crumbled feta cheese
1 (6 ounces) jar roasted red peppers, drained, and chopped
1 (10 ounces) jar dolmans (grape leaves), drained and rinsed (optional)

Directions: In a large mixing bowl, whisk together the olive oil, oregano, vinegar, and garlic until fully combined. Add the black olives, chickpeas, artichoke hearts, capers, feta cheese, and roasted red peppers to the bowl. Toss until everything is well coated in the dressing. If using the dolmans, chop them into small pieces and add them to the bowl. Toss again until everything is well mixed. Cover the bowl with plastic wrap and refrigerate for at least an hour to allow the flavors to meld. Serve the salad chilled or at room temperature, either on its own or over a bed of lettuce.

Nutrition: Calories: 394, Fat: 29g, Protein: 11g, Carbohydrates: 29g, Fiber: 8g, Sodium: 1064mg

Barley Salad with Lemon Tahini Dressing

Preparation time: 15 minutes **Cooking time:** 10 minutes **Serves** 4 to 6

Ingredients:
1½ cups pearl barley
5 tbsp extravirgin olive oil, divided
1½ tsp s table salt, for cooking barley
¼ cup tahini
1 tsp grated lemon zest plus ¼ cup juice (2 lemons)
1 tbsp sumac, divided
1 garlic clove, minced
¾ tsp table salt

1 English cucumber, cut into ½inch pieces
1 carrot, peeled and shredded
1 red bell pepper, stemmed, seeded, and chopped
4 scallions, sliced thin
2 tbsp finely chopped jarred hot cherry peppers
¼ cup coarsely chopped fresh mint

Directions: Bring a pot of water to a boil. Add the barley and 1 1/2 teaspoons of salt and cook until the barley is tender, about 30 minutes. Drain the barley and let it cool to room temperature. Meanwhile, in a small bowl, whisk together the tahini, lemon zest, lemon juice, 1/2 tablespoon of sumac, garlic, 3/4 teaspoon of salt, and 2 tablespoons of water until smooth. In a large bowl, toss together the cooked barley, cucumber, carrot, bell pepper, scallions, and cherry peppers. Add the dressing and toss until everything is evenly coated. Transfer the salad to a serving platter and sprinkle with the remaining 1/2 tablespoon of sumac and the fresh mint. Serve immediately, or refrigerate until ready to serve.

Nutrition: Calories: 370, fat: 18g, protein: 8g, carbs: 47g, fiber: 10g, sodium: 510mg

Mediterranean Salad with Bulgur

Preparation time: 27 minutes **Cooking time:** 12 minutes **Serves** 4

Ingredients:
1 cup water
½ cup dried bulgur
1 (9ounce / 255g) bag chopped romaine lettuce
1 English cucumber, cut into ¼inchthick slices
1 red bell pepper, chopped
½ cup raw hulled pumpkin seeds
20 kalamata olives, pitted and halved lengthwise
¼ cup extravirgin olive oil
Juice of 1 small orange
Juice of 1 small lemon
¼ tsp dried oregano
Sea salt
Freshly ground black pepper

Directions: Bring the water to a boil in a small saucepan. Add the bulgur and a pinch of salt, reduce the heat to low, and simmer for about 15 minutes, or until the water is absorbed and the bulgur is tender. Remove from the heat and let cool. In a large salad bowl, combine the cooked bulgur, romaine lettuce, cucumber slices, red bell pepper, pumpkin seeds, and olives. In a small bowl, whisk together the olive oil, orange juice, lemon juice, oregano, salt, and pepper. Pour the dressing over the salad and toss to combine. Serve the salad immediately, garnished with additional salt and pepper to taste.

Nutrition: Calories: 322, fat: 23g, protein: 8g, carbs: 24g, fiber: 6g, sodium: 262mg

Roasted Cauliflower Salad with Tahini-Yogurt Dressing

Preparation time: 10 minutes **Cooking time:** 30 minutes **Serves** 8 to 10

Ingredients:
10 cups cauliflower florets (1 to 2inch florets, from 1 to 2 heads) 1½ tbsp olive oil
¾ tsp kosher salt, divided
½ cup walnuts
½ cup yogurt
¼ cup tahini, at room temperature
¼ cup lemon juice, plus more to taste
¼ cup water

1 tbsp honey
¼ cup chopped fresh dill
1 tbsp minced shallot

Directions: Preheat your oven to 425°F (220°C). On a large baking sheet, toss the cauliflower florets with the olive oil and 1/2 teaspoon of the salt. Roast for 20 to 25 minutes, or until tender and lightly browned. Meanwhile, toast the walnuts in a small dry skillet over medium heat until fragrant and lightly browned, about 5 minutes. In a small bowl, whisk together the yogurt, tahini, lemon juice, water, honey, and the remaining 1/4 teaspoon of salt until smooth. In a large serving bowl, combine the roasted cauliflower, toasted walnuts, dill, and shallot. Drizzle with the tahini-yogurt dressing and toss to coat. Serve immediately.

Nutrition: Calories: 153, fat: 10g, protein: 6g, carbs: 12g, fiber: 4g, sodium: 249mg

Spinach Salad with Citrus Vinaigrette

Prep Time: 10 minutes **Cook time:** 0 minutes **Serves** 4

CITRUS VINAIGRETTE:
1 pound (454 g) baby spinach, washed, stems removed
1 large ripe tomato, cut into ¼ inch pieces
1 medium red onion, thinly sliced
For the vinaigrette:

¼ cup extra virgin olive oil
3 tablespoons balsamic vinegar
½ teaspoon fresh lemon zest
½ teaspoon salt

In a small bowl, whisk together the olive oil, balsamic vinegar, lemon zest, and salt. In a large salad bowl, combine the spinach, tomato, and red onion. Drizzle the vinaigrette over the salad and toss to coat. Serve immediately.

Nutrition: Calories: 173, total fat: 14.2g, saturated fat: 2.2g, total carbs: 10.2g, fiber: 4.2g, protein: 4.1g, sugar: 2.2g, sodium: 388mg, cholesterol: 0mg

Balsamic Chicken Pasta and Salad

Prep Time: 15 minutes **Cooking Time:** 20 minutes **Total Time:** 35 minutes **Servings:** 4

Ingredients:
3 1/2 cups uncooked butterfly pasta
4 1/2 cups diced cooked chicken breast
1/3 cup balsamic vinegar
2 cups tomatoes, diced
1/2 cup red onion, diced
1/4 cup fresh Gorgonzola cheese, crumbled
1/2 cup Parmesan cheese, shredded
1 tsp. garlic, chopped
1/2 cup extra virgin olive oil
1/4 cup chopped fresh basil
6 tsp. brown sugar
1/4 tsp. kosher salt and 1/4 tsp. black pepper

Directions: Start by boiling some water and cooking the pasta according to the package instructions. While the pasta is cooking, you can dice up some cooked chicken breast and set it aside. In a separate bowl, mix together the balsamic vinegar, diced tomatoes, diced red onion, crumbled Gorgonzola cheese, and shredded Parmesan cheese. Set this mixture aside. Once the pasta is cooked, drain it and return it to the pot. Add in the diced chicken, tomato and cheese mixture, and chopped garlic. Drizzle the pasta with extra virgin olive oil and sprinkle with chopped basil, brown sugar, salt, and pepper. Toss everything together until the pasta is evenly coated with the dressing and ingredients.

Nutrition per serving: Calories: 728, Fat: 37g, Saturated Fat: 8g, Cholesterol: 127mg, Sodium: 740mg, Carbohydrates: 58g, Fiber: 3g, Sugar: 14g, Protein: 39g.

Simple Celery and Orange Salad

Prep Time: 15 minutes   **Cook time:** 0 minutes **Serves** 6

SALAD:
3 celery stalks, including leaves, sliced diagonally into ½inch slices
½ cup green olives
¼ cup sliced red onion
2 large peeled oranges, cut into rounds
Dressing:
1 tablespoon extravirgin olive oil
1 tablespoon freshly squeezed lemon or orange juice
1 tablespoon olive brine
¼ teaspoon kosher or sea salt
¼ teaspoon freshly ground black pepper

Directions: In a small bowl, whisk together the ingredients for the dressing: olive oil, lemon or orange juice, olive brine, salt, and pepper. In a large salad bowl, combine the celery, green olives, red onion, and orange slices. Pour the dressing over the salad and toss to coat everything evenly. Serve the salad immediately, garnished with a sprinkle of salt and pepper, if desired.

Nutrition per Serving: Calories: 24, total fat: 1.2g, saturated fat: 0g, total carbs: 2.2g, fiber: 1.2g, protein: 1.1g, sugar: 2.3g, sodium: 135mg, phosphorus: 5mg, potassium: 52mg, cholesterol: 2mg

Rice & Lentil Salad with Caramelized Onions

Servings:4 **Cooking Time:**1 Hour 15 Minutes

Ingredients:
1 cup brown rice
2 cups lentils
¼ cup olive oil
4 ½ cups water
½ tsp dried thyme
½ tsp dried tarragon
3 onions, peeled and sliced
Salt and black pepper to taste

Directions: Rinse the brown rice and lentils in a fine mesh strainer under cold running water. In a large pot, bring the water to a boil. Add the rice and lentils, and reduce the heat to low. Cover the pot and simmer for 45 minutes, or until the water is absorbed and the rice and lentils are tender. In a separate pan, heat the olive oil over medium heat. Add the sliced onions and cook, stirring frequently, until they are caramelized and golden brown, about 20-30 minutes. Once the rice and lentils are cooked, transfer them to a large mixing bowl. Add the caramelized onions, thyme, tarragon, and salt and pepper to taste. Stir until everything is evenly combined. Serve the salad warm or chilled.

Nutrition per Serving: Calories: 498; Fat: 19g; Protein: 15g; Carbs: 63g.

Shredded Zucchini Salad

Prep Time: 10 minutes **Cook time:** 0 minutes **Serves** 2

Ingredients:
1 medium zucchini, shredded or sliced paper thin

6 halved cherry tomatoes
3 tablespoons olive oil
Juice of 1 lemon
Sea salt and freshly ground black pepper, to taste
3 to 4 basil leaves, thinly sliced
2 tablespoons Parmesan cheese, grated

Directions: Begin by shredding your zucchini using a grater or a mandoline slicer. If using a grater, be sure to use the largest holes for shredding. If using a mandoline, slice the zucchini as thinly as possible. In a small bowl, whisk together the olive oil, lemon juice, salt, and pepper to create the dressing. In a large bowl, toss together the shredded zucchini, cherry tomatoes, and basil. Pour the dressing over the top and toss to evenly coat the vegetables. Sprinkle the grated Parmesan cheese over the top of the salad and serve immediately.

Nutrition: Calories: 55, total fat: 21g, saturated fat: 3.5g, total carbs: 2.5g, fiber: 0.1g, protein: 1.7g, sugar: 0.6g, sodium: 91mg, phosphorus: 38mg, potassium: 59mg, cholesterol: 4mg

French-Style Dressing for Greek Salad

Prep Time: 10 minutes **Cooking Time:** 0 minutes **Additional Time:** 0 minutes **Total Time:** 10 minutes **Servings:** 4

Ingredients:
1/2 cup of extra virgin olive oil
1 garlic clove, crushed
1/4 cup of wine vinegar
1 tbsp. of lemon juice
1 tsp. of lemon zest grated
1/4 tsp. of ground black pepper
1/4 tsp. of white sugar
1/4 tsp. of Dijon mustard
1 tbsp. of water

Directions: In a small bowl, whisk together the olive oil, crushed garlic, wine vinegar, lemon juice, grated lemon zest, black pepper, sugar, and Dijon mustard. Add in the water and whisk until fully combined. Set aside. Next, prepare your Greek salad. You can use any combination of ingredients that you like, such as crisp lettuce, juicy tomatoes, thinly sliced red onions, crumbled feta cheese, and olives. Toss the salad ingredients together in a large bowl. Finally, drizzle the French-Style Dressing over the top of the salad and toss until everything is evenly coated. Serve immediately, garnished with a sprinkle of additional feta cheese and a sprig of fresh herbs, if desired.

Nutrition: calories 240, fat 27g, carbohydrate 4g, protein 0g

Antipasto Salad

Prep Time: 15 minutes **Cooking Time:** 0 minutes **Total Time:** 15 minutes **Servings:** 6
Ingredients:
13 oz. artichoke hearts, quartered
1/2 cup halved cherry tomatoes
1/4 cup roasted red peppers, diced
1/2 cup halved green olives
1/2 cup black olives
1/2 lemon juice
1/2 cup mozzarella, balls
8 oz. provolone cheese, cubed
3 cups romaine, diced
8 oz. Genoa salami, cubed
1/2 cup olive oil

1/2 cup mini pepperoni
1 tsp. Italian seasoning

Directions: In a large bowl, combine the artichoke hearts, cherry tomatoes, roasted red peppers, green olives, black olives, and lemon juice. Add the mozzarella cheese balls, provolone cheese, romaine lettuce, and Genoa salami to the bowl and toss to combine. In a small bowl, whisk together the olive oil, mini pepperoni, and Italian seasoning to create the dressing. Pour the dressing over the salad and toss to coat evenly. Serve the salad immediately, or refrigerate until ready to serve.

Nutrition per serving: calories 433, fat 66g, carbohydrates 8g, protein 49g

Chicken Salad Caprese

Prep Time: 40 minutes **Cooking Time:** 5 minutes **Total Time:** 45 minutes **Servings:** 6
Ingredients:
2 cups grated rotisserie chicken
1 1/2 lb. mozzarella cheese, diced
2 1/2 cups grape tomatoes, cut in half
16 oz. can of waterpacked artichoke hearts, soakdrain, coarsely diced
1 1/2 cups pitted Greek olives, finely sliced
2 garlic cloves, chopped
1/4 cup fresh basil, chopped
1/4 cup extra virgin olive oil
1/2 tsp. kosher salt
1/2 tsp. black pepper
Crostini:
4 garlic cloves
23 French bread baguettes
1/4 cup extra virgin olive oil
1 tsp. kosher salt

Directions: Preheat your oven to 400ºF. In a small bowl, mix together the minced garlic, olive oil, and salt. Brush this mixture onto both sides of the bread slices, then place them on a baking sheet. Bake the bread slices for 5-7 minutes, or until they are lightly toasted. Remove from the oven and set aside to cool. In a large bowl, combine the shredded chicken, diced mozzarella, halved grape tomatoes, diced artichoke hearts, sliced olives, chopped garlic, and chopped basil. In a separate small bowl, whisk together the olive oil, kosher salt, and black pepper. Pour this dressing over the chicken salad mixture and toss to coat everything evenly. Arrange the toasted bread slices on a serving platter and spoon the chicken salad caprese on top. Garnish with additional basil leaves, if desired. Serve immediately.

Nutrition per serving: calories: 447, fat: 28g, carbohydrates: 37,5g, protein: 32g

Greek Beef Salad

Prep Time: 20 minutes **Cooking Time:** 15 minutes **Total Time:** 35 minutes **Servings:** 4
Ingredients:
1 1/2 lb. beef steak
6 cups lettuce
2 tbsp. crumbled feta cheese
1 medium cucumber
1/2 red onion
2 pita pieces of bread
2 cups lemon juice
2 tsp. dried oregano
1 cup olive oil
1/2 tsp. salt

1/2 tsp. black pepper

Directions: To start, preheat your grill or broiler to high heat. Season your beef steak with salt, pepper, and oregano, and grill or broil until it reaches your desired level of doneness. While the steak is cooking, slice your cucumber and red onion into thin rounds. Once the steak is cooked, remove it from the grill or broiler and let it rest for a few minutes to allow the juices to redistribute. In the meantime, toast your pita bread until it is crispy and slightly charred. To assemble the salad, place your lettuce in a large bowl or on a platter. Top with the sliced cucumber, red onion, and feta cheese. Cut the steak into thin slices and arrange on top of the salad. Drizzle with a mixture of lemon juice, olive oil, and a pinch of salt and pepper. Finish the salad off with a sprinkle of oregano and serve immediately, accompanied by the crispy toasted pita bread.

Nutrition per serving: calories: 278, fat: 20g, carbohydrates: 9,5g, protein: 17g

Asparagus & Goat Cheese Rice Salad

Servings:4 **Cooking Time:**35 Minutes

Ingredients:
3 tbsp olive oil
½ cups brown rice
Salt and black pepper to taste
½ lemon, zested and juiced
1 lb asparagus, chopped
1 shallot, minced
2 oz goat cheese, crumbled
¼ cup hazelnuts, toasted
¼ cup parsley, minced

Directions: Heat 2 tablespoons of olive oil in a medium saucepan over medium heat. Add the brown rice, season with salt and pepper, and cook for about 20 minutes, or until the rice is tender and has absorbed all of the water. While the rice is cooking, prepare the asparagus by chopping it into 1-inch pieces and blanching it in a pot of boiling water for 2-3 minutes. Drain the asparagus and set it aside. In a large bowl, whisk together the remaining 1 tablespoon of olive oil, the lemon zest and juice, and the minced shallot. When the rice is done cooking, add it to the bowl with the asparagus, goat cheese, hazelnuts, and parsley. Toss everything together until the ingredients are evenly distributed. Serve the salad immediately, garnished with additional goat cheese and parsley if desired.

Nutrition per Serving: Calories: 185; Fat: 16g; Protein: 8g; Carbs: 24g.

SOUPS AND STEWS

Traditional Meatball Soup

Servings:6 **Cooking Time:** 50 Minutes

Ingredients:
2 tbsp olive oil
1 can diced tomatoes
½ cup rice, rinsed
12 oz ground beef
2 shallots, chopped
1 tbsp dried thyme
1 carrot, chopped
1 tsp garlic powder
5 garlic cloves, minced

6 cups chicken broth
¼ cup chopped basil leaves
Salt and black pepper to taste.

Directions: In a large pot or Dutch oven, heat the olive oil over medium heat. Add the shallots, carrot, and garlic and cook until the vegetables are soft, about 5 minutes. Add the ground beef to the pot and cook until it's browned, breaking it up into small pieces as it cooks. Add the diced tomatoes, thyme, and rice to the pot and stir to combine. Pour in the chicken broth and bring the mixture to a boil. Reduce the heat to low and let the soup simmer for 30 minutes, or until the rice is cooked and the flavors have melded together. Using a small cookie scoop or spoon, shape the ground beef mixture into small meatballs and add them to the soup. Let the meatballs cook in the soup for an additional 10 minutes, or until they're cooked through. Stir in the chopped basil and season the soup with salt and black pepper to taste. Serve the soup hot, garnished with additional chopped basil if desired.

Nutrition per Serving: Calories: 265; Fat: 9.8g; Protein: 24g; Carbs: 19g.

Goat Cheese & Beet Salad with Nuts
Servings:4 **Cooking Time**:10 Minutes

Ingredients:
3 steamed beets, cut into wedges
3 tbsp olive oil
Salt and black pepper to taste
2 tbsp lime juice
4 oz goat cheese, crumbled
1/3 cup hazelnuts, chopped
1 tbsp chives, chopped

Directions: Begin by heating your oven to 400°F (200°C) and lightly oiling a baking sheet. Place the beet wedges on the sheet and roast until tender, about 20-25 minutes. Let them cool before cutting into bite-sized pieces. In a small bowl, whisk together the olive oil, lime juice, salt, and pepper to make the dressing. In a large salad bowl, combine the beets, goat cheese, hazelnuts, and chives. Drizzle the dressing over the top and toss gently to coat. Serve immediately

Nutrition per serving: Calories: 160; Fat: 5g; Protein: 5g; Carbs: 7g.

Garden Veggie Soup
Time: 30 minutes **Servings**:5

Ingredients:
4 Roma tomatoes, cored and diced
3 cloves garlic, minced
1 yellow onion, chopped
1 red bell pepper, seeded and sliced
2 large carrots, sliced
2 tablespoons fresh basil, chopped
2 large potatoes, chopped
1 celery, chopped
2 tablespoons olive oil
5 cups vegetable broth
1/2 teaspoon red pepper flakes, crushed
1 bay leaf
2 tablespoons fresh parsley, chopped
½ teaspoon salt
½ teaspoon pepper

Directions: In a large pot or Dutch oven, heat the olive oil over medium heat. Add the onion, garlic, and red pepper and cook for about 5 minutes, or until the vegetables are softened. Add the tomatoes, carrots, potatoes, celery, basil, red pepper flakes, bay leaf, salt, and pepper. Stir well to combine. Pour in the vegetable broth and bring the mixture to a boil. Reduce the heat to low and simmer for about 20 minutes, or until the vegetables are tender. Remove the bay leaf and discard. Stir in the parsley. Serve the soup hot, garnished with a sprinkle of fresh parsley if desired.

Nutrition per serving: Calories 209; Fat 7.5g; Carbs 32.3g; Protein 4.7g; Sugars 4.7g

Creamy Mushroom Soup
Ready in about 35 minutes **Servings** 6

Ingredients:
1 lb. Cremini mushrooms, chopped
½ teaspoon salt
4 tablespoons butter
1/2 cup yellow onion, diced
½ lb. Portobello mushrooms, chopped
3 carrots, sliced
2 cloves garlic, minced
1 ½ teaspoon fresh thyme
½ teaspoon pepper
5 cups vegetable broth
½ teaspoon pepper
2 tablespoons plain flour

Directions: In a pot, melt the butter over medium heat. Add the onions, carrots, and garlic and sauté until the onions are translucent, about 5 minutes. Add the Cremini and Portobello mushrooms and cook for an additional 5 minutes, until the mushrooms are soft. Stir in the thyme, salt, and pepper. Add the vegetable broth and bring to a boil. Reduce the heat to low and simmer for 20 minutes. In a small bowl, whisk together the flour and 1 cup of water until smooth. Slowly pour the flour mixture into the soup, stirring constantly, until the soup thickens. Remove the soup from the heat and let it cool for a few minutes before serving. Garnish with fresh thyme and a sprinkle of black pepper.

Nutrition per serving: 179 Calories; 13.5g Fat; 11.8g Carbs; 6.7g Protein; 4.6g Sugars

Spelt Soup
Preparation time: 10 minutes **Cooking time:** 30 minutes **Servings:** 4

Ingredients
2 cups pearl spelt (or spelt precooked canned)
1 carrot, chopped
1 celery rib, chopped
7-8 cherry tomatoes, halved
1/2 white onion, diced
3 tablespoons extra virgin olive oil
4 cups hot vegetable broth
salt, to taste

Directions: Heat the olive oil in a large pot over medium heat. Add the onion, carrot, and celery and sauté until the vegetables are soft and translucent, about 5-7 minutes. Add the cherry tomatoes and continue to cook for another 2-3 minutes. Pour in enough hot broth to cover the vegetables and bring to a boil. Add the spelt and return to a boil. Reduce the heat to low and simmer for 20-25 minutes, or until the spelt is tender. Season with salt to taste and serve hot.

Nutrition per serving: Calories: 250, Total fat: 11 g, Saturated fat: 1.5 g, Cholesterol: 0 mg, Sodium: 360 mg, Total carbohydrate: 30 g, Dietary fiber: 5 g, Sugar: 6 g, Protein: 10 g

Greek Tomato Soup with Orzo

Preparation Time: 15 minutes **Cooking Time**: 20 minutes **Servings**: 1

Ingredients:
2 tablespoons olive oil
1 medium onion, chopped
1/4 teaspoon salt
1/4 teaspoon pepper
Crumbled feta cheese and minced fresh basil (Optional)
11/3 cups uncooked whole wheat orzo pasta
2 cans (141/2 ounces each) whole tomatoes, undrained, coarsely chopped
3 cups reduced sodium chicken broth
2 teaspoons dried oregano

Directions: In a large saucepan, heat oil over medium heat. Add onion; cook and stir until tender. Add salt and pepper. Stir in the orzo, tomatoes, broth, and oregano. Bring to a boil. Reduce heat; simmer, uncovered, for 15 minutes or until orzo is tender. Serve with feta cheese and basil if desired.

Nutrition per serving: Calories: 199, Fat: 5g, Cholesterol: 5mg, Sodium: 434mg, Carbohydrates: 31g, Fiber: 3g, Protein: 7g

Tomato Seafood Soup

Servings: 4 **Cooking Time**: 20 Minutes

Ingredients:
½ lb cod, skinless and cubed
2 tbsp olive oil
½ lb shrimp, deveined
1 yellow onion, chopped
1 carrot, finely chopped
1 celery stalk, finely chopped
1 small pepper, chopped
1 garlic clove, minced
½ cup tomatoes, crushed
4 cups fish stock
¼ tsp rosemary, dried
Salt and black pepper to taste

Directions: Heat the olive oil in a large pot over medium heat. Add the onion, carrot, celery, and pepper to the pot and sauté until the vegetables are soft, about 5-7 minutes. Add the minced garlic to the pot and cook for an additional minute. Pour in the crushed tomatoes and fish stock, and bring the mixture to a boil. Reduce the heat to low and simmer the soup for 10 minutes. Add the cod and shrimp to the pot and cook until the seafood is cooked through, about 5-7 minutes. Season the soup with rosemary, salt, and black pepper to taste. Serve the soup hot and garnish with fresh herbs if desired.

Nutrition per serving: Calories: 200; Fat: 9g; Protein: 27g; Carbs: 5g.

Butternut Squash and Beef Stew

Preparation time: 15 minutes **Cooking time:** 35 minutes **Servings:** 4

Ingredients:
3 teaspoons olive oil
1 pound (454 g) ground beef
1 cup beef stock
14 ounces (397 g) canned tomatoes with juice

1 tablespoon stevia
1 pound (454 g) butternut squash, chopped
1 tablespoon Worcestershire sauce
2 bay leaves
Salt and black pepper, to taste
1 onion, chopped
1 teaspoon dried sage
1 tablespoon garlic, minced

Directions: Heat 1 teaspoon of the olive oil in a large pot over medium heat. Add the ground beef and cook until browned, about 5-7 minutes. Remove the beef from the pot and set aside. In the same pot, heat the remaining 2 teaspoons of olive oil. Add the onion, garlic, and squash. Cook for 3-4 minutes, or until the vegetables are slightly softened. Add the beef stock, canned tomatoes, stevia, Worcestershire sauce, bay leaves, salt, and pepper to the pot. Bring the mixture to a boil, then reduce the heat to low and simmer for 15-20 minutes. Add the cooked beef back to the pot and continue to simmer for an additional 5-10 minutes, or until the squash is tender. Serve the stew hot, garnished with dried sage and a sprinkle of black pepper.

Nutrition: calories: 342, fat: 17.1g, protein: 31.9g, carbs: 11.6g, net carbs: 7.4g, fiber: 4.2g

Moroccan Lentil Soup

Preparation time: 10 minutes **Cooking time:** 65 minutes **Servings:** 4
Ingredients:
1 tbsp. extravirgin olive oil
1 c. chopped onion
1 c. chopped celery
½ c. chopped carrot
2 garlic cloves, minced
2 tsps. ground cumin
2 tsps. smoked paprika
1 tsp salt
1 tsp freshly ground black pepper
1 tsp ground turmeric
1 tsp ground ginger
½ tsp ground cinnamon
4 c. chicken broth
2 c. water
2 tbsps. tomato paste
2 c. brown lentils
¼ c. nonfat plain Greek yogurt
Chopped fresh flatleaf parsley, for garnish

Directions: Heat the olive oil in a large pot over medium heat. Add the onion, celery, carrot, and garlic and cook until the vegetables are soft, about 5 minutes. Add the cumin, paprika, salt, pepper, turmeric, ginger, and cinnamon to the pot and stir to coat the vegetables. Cook for an additional 2 minutes, until the spices are fragrant. Add the chicken broth, water, and tomato paste to the pot and stir to combine. Bring the mixture to a boil, then reduce the heat to low and simmer for 20 minutes. Add the lentils to the pot and simmer for an additional 20 minutes, or until the lentils are tender. Stir in the Greek yogurt and heat until warmed through. Garnish with chopped parsley and serve hot.

Nutrition per serving: calories 273, fat 7,75 g, carbohydrates 42g, protein 16,25g

Sausage & Cannellini Bean Soup

Preparation Time: 15 minutes **Cooking Time:** 20 minutes **Servings:** 1
Ingredients:

3 Italian turkey sausage links (4 ounces each), casings removed
1/4 cup white wine
1/4 teaspoon pepper
One bunch escarole or spinach, chopped
Four teaspoons shredded Parmesan cheese
One medium onion, chopped
Two garlic cloves, minced
One can (15 ounces) cannellini beans, rinsed and drained
One can (141/2 ounces) reduced-sodium chicken broth 1 cup water

Directions: Heat a large soup pot over medium-high heat. Add the sausage and cook, stirring occasionally, until it is browned and crumbled. Add the wine, pepper, escarole or spinach, Parmesan cheese, onion, and garlic to the pot. Cook, stirring occasionally, until the vegetables are tender. Add the beans, chicken broth, and water to the pot. Bring the mixture to a boil, then reduce the heat to low and simmer for 10 minutes. Serve the soup hot, garnished with additional Parmesan cheese if desired.

Nutrition: Calories: 547, Fat: 15g, Saturated Fat: 4g, Cholesterol: 88mg, Sodium: 1073mg, Carbohydrates: 60g, Fiber: 8g, Sugar: 6g, Protein: 41g.

Fish Stew with Tomatoes and Olives
Serves: 4 **Time**: 25 minutes

Ingredients:
1/2 lb. halibut filet
4 cloves garlic, minced
1 cup cherry tomatoes, hamper the centre
3 cups tomato soup
1 cup green olives, hollowed and cut

Directions: Heat the olive oil in a large pot over medium heat. Add the garlic and sauté until fragrant, about 1 minute. Add the cherry tomatoes, tomato soup, and green olives to the pot. Bring the mixture to a boil, then reduce the heat to low and simmer for 10 minutes. Add the halibut to the pot and cook until the fish is fully cooked and flaky, about 5-7 minutes. Season the stew with oregano, salt, and pepper to taste. Serve hot.

Nutrition: Calories 245, Total Fat 3.7g, Saturated Fat 0.6g, Cholesterol 35mg, Sodium 1098mg, Total Carbohydrate 28g, Dietary Fibre 2.9g, Total Sugars 16.5g, Protein 26.3g, Potassium 1040mg

Flavorful Meatball Soup
Preparation Time: 15 minutes **Cooking Time:** 20 minutes **Servings:** 1

Ingredients:
Two celery ribs, chopped
15 fresh baby carrots, chopped
One small onion, chopped
One can (15 ounces) cannellini beans, rinsed and drained
One can (141/2 ounces) Italian diced tomatoes, undrained
One can (141/2 ounces) reducedsodium chicken broth
3/4 cup chopped cabbage
3/4 cup cut fresh green beans
3 tablespoons shredded partskim mozzarella cheese
1 pound lean ground turkey
21/2 teaspoons Italian seasoning, divided
1/4 teaspoon paprika
1/4 teaspoon salt, divided
1/4 teaspoon coarsely ground pepper, divided
Four teaspoons olive oil, divided

Directions: In a large saucepan, heat 2 teaspoons olive oil over medium heat. Add the celery, carrots, and onion; cook and stir for 3-4 minutes or until tender. Add the beans, tomatoes, broth, cabbage, and green beans. Bring to a boil. Reduce heat; simmer for 5 minutes or until vegetables are tender. Meanwhile, in a large bowl, combine the cheese, turkey, 1 1/2 teaspoons Italian seasoning, paprika, 1/8 teaspoon salt, and 1/8 teaspoon pepper. Shape into 1-inch balls. In a large skillet, heat the remaining olive oil over medium heat. Add the meatballs; cook and stir for 5-7 minutes or until browned. Add the meatballs to the soup; simmer for 5 minutes or until heated through. Stir in the remaining Italian seasoning and salt. Sprinkle with mozzarella cheese before serving.

Nutrition: Calories: 528, Fat: 24g, Cholesterol: 95mg, Sodium: 1291mg, Carbohydrates: 47g, Fiber: 10g, Protein: 31g

Roman Oxtail Stew

Preparation time: 15 minutes **Cooking time:** 2 hours and 30 minutes **Servings:** 6

Ingredients:
¼ cup olive oil
4 pounds oxtails, about 1½ inches thick
1 large onion, chopped
2 garlic cloves, chopped
1 cup dry red wine
1 28ounce can of Italian peeled tomatoes with their juice
¼ teaspoon of ground cloves
Salt and freshly ground pepper
6 medium celery ribs, sliced
1 tablespoon chopped bittersweet chocolate
2 tablespoons pine nuts
2 tablespoons raisins

Directions: Heat the olive oil in a large pot over medium heat. Add the oxtails and brown them on all sides, about 8 minutes. Add the onion and garlic and cook until the onion is translucent, about 5 minutes. Pour in the wine and bring it to a boil, scraping the bottom of the pot to release any browned bits. Stir in the tomatoes and their juice, along with the ground cloves, salt, and pepper. Add the celery, chocolate, pine nuts, and raisins. Reduce the heat to low and simmer, uncovered, until the oxtails are tender, about 2 hours. Serve hot and enjoy!

Nutrition: Calories: 233, Carbs: 19g, Fat: 12g, Protein: 13g

Mediterranean Vegetable Stew

Prep time: 15 minutes **Cook time:** 35 minutes **Serving:** 4

Ingredients:
Olive oil, divided, 2 tablespoons
Red onion, 1 cup
Green pepper, 2 cups
Garlic cloves, crushed, 2
Sliced mushrooms, 1 cup
Small eggplant, 1
Crushed tomatoes, 1 can
Kalamata olives, ½ cup
Chickpeas, 1 can
Chopped fresh rosemary, 1 tablespoon
Coarsely chopped parsley, 1 cup

Directions: Heat 1 tablespoon of olive oil in a pot over medium heat. Add the onion, green pepper, and garlic and cook until the vegetables are tender, about 5 minutes. Add the mushrooms and eggplant to the pot and cook for an additional 5 minutes. Pour in the crushed tomatoes and add the Kalamata olives, chickpeas, and rosemary. Stir. Bring the stew to a boil, then reduce the heat to low and simmer for 20 minutes, or until the vegetables are tender. Stir in the parsley and serve hot.

Nutrition: Calories: 199, Fat: 9g, Saturated fat: 1g, Cholesterol: 0mg, Sodium: 621mg, Carbohydrates: 26g, Fiber: 7g, Sugar: 9g, Protein: 6g

Springtime Veal Stew

Preparation time: 15 minutes **Cooking time:** 2 hours **Servings:** 6

Ingredients:
3 large carrots, cut into ¼inchthick slices
2 medium onions, chopped
3 tablespoons olive oil
1 garlic clove, finely chopped
2 teaspoons chopped fresh rosemary
2 pounds veal shoulder or chuck, trimmed and cut into 2inch pieces 2 cups Chicken Broth
2 tablespoons tomato paste
Salt and freshly ground pepper
4 cups of water
1 cup asparagus, 1inch pieces
1 cup thawed frozen green peas or baby lima beans

Directions: In a large pot or Dutch oven, heat 2 tablespoons of olive oil over medium-high heat. Add the veal and cook until it's browned on all sides, about 8-10 minutes. Remove the veal from the pot and set aside. In the same pot, add the remaining 1 tablespoon of olive oil and the onions, garlic, and carrots. Cook for about 5 minutes, until the vegetables are softened. Add the veal back into the pot along with the chicken broth, tomato paste, salt, and pepper. Bring the mixture to a boil. Reduce the heat to low and let the stew simmer for about 1 hour, or until the veal is tender. Add the asparagus, green peas, and rosemary to the pot and continue to simmer for an additional 15 minutes. Serve the stew hot, garnished with chopped parsley if desired.

Nutrition: Calories: 280 Carbs: 31g Fat: 4g Protein: 32g

Red Lentil Soup Mix

Preparation Time: 15 minutes **Cooking Time:** 40 minutes **Servings:** 1

Ingredients:
1/4 cup dried minced onion
2 tbsp dried parsley flakes
2 tsp ground allspice
1 tsp pepper
1/2 tsp ground cloves
2 packages (1 lb each) dried red lentils
Additional ingredients (for each batch):
1 medium carrot, finely chopped
1 celery rib, finely chopped
1 tbsp olive oil
2 cans (141/2 ounces each) vegetable broth
2 tsp ground cumin
2 tsp ground turmeric
1 1/2 tsp salt
1 tsp garlic powder
1 tsp ground cardamom
1 tsp ground cinnamon

Directions: In a large mixing bowl, combine the dried minced onion, parsley flakes, allspice, pepper, and ground cloves. Stir in the dried red lentils until they are evenly coated in the seasoning mix. Transfer the soup mix to an airtight container or sealable bag. Label the container with the additional ingredients needed for each batch. When ready to prepare the soup, heat the olive oil in a large pot over medium heat. Add the chopped carrot and celery and sauté for 5 minutes, or until they are tender. Stir in the vegetable broth, cumin, turmeric, salt, garlic powder, cardamom, and cinnamon. Bring the mixture to a boil. Add the soup mix to the pot and reduce the heat to low. Simmer the soup for 20-30 minutes, or until the lentils are tender. Serve the soup hot, garnished with chopped fresh herbs or a sprinkle of Parmesan cheese, if desired.

Nutrition: Calories 1560, Fat 16g, Carbohydrate 282g, Protein 112g

Pumpkin soup

Serves: 4 **Cooking Time**: 35 minutes

Ingredients:
1 onion, hacked
2 cups yam, hacked
30 oz. pumpkin puree
1quart chicken broth
1 teaspoon garlic powder

Directions: Heat a large pot over medium heat and add in 1 tablespoon of olive oil. Once the oil is hot, add in 1 hacked onion and sauté until it becomes translucent, about 5 minutes. Next, add in 2 cups of hacked yam and sauté for an additional 3 minutes. Then, stir in 30 ounces of pumpkin puree and 1 quart of chicken broth. Bring the mixture to a boil, then reduce the heat to a simmer and let it cook for 20 minutes. Finally, stir in 1 teaspoon of garlic powder and let the soup simmer for an additional 5 minutes. Serve the soup hot, garnished with a sprinkle of chopped fresh herbs if desired.

Nutrition: Calories 186, Total Fat 1.4g, Saturated Fat 0.5g, Cholesterol 0mg, Sodium 812mg, Total Carbohydrate 41.7g, Dietary Fibre 10.2g, Total Sugars 15.6g, Protein 5.5g, Potassium 976mg

Country-Style Chicken Stew

Preparation Time: 20 minutes **Cooking Time**: 1 hour **Servings**: 6

Ingredients:
1 pound chicken thighs
2 tablespoons butter, room temperature
1/2 pound carrots, chopped
1 bell pepper, chopped
1 chili pepper, deveined and minced
1 cup tomato puree
Kosher salt and ground black pepper
1/2 teaspoon smoked paprika
1 onion, finely chopped
1 teaspoon garlic, sliced
4 cups vegetable broth
1 teaspoon dried basil
1 celery, chopped

Directions: Preheat a pot over medium heat. Add the butter and let it melt. Season the chicken thighs with salt, pepper, and paprika. Place them in the pot and brown them on both sides for about 4-5 minutes per side. Remove the chicken from the pot and set it aside. Add the chopped onion, garlic, and chili pepper to the pot and sauté for 2-3 minutes, until the onions are translucent. Add the carrot, bell pepper, and celery to the pot and cook for an additional 3-4 minutes. Add the tomato puree, vegetable broth, and dried basil to the pot and bring the mixture to a boil. Reduce the heat to low and return the chicken to the pot. Cover the pot with a lid and simmer for 30-35 minutes, until the chicken is cooked through and the vegetables are tender. Serve the stew hot, garnished with fresh chopped herbs.

Nutrition: Calories 280, Fat 14.7g, Carbs 2.5g, Protein 25.6g, Fiber 2.5g

Zucchini Cacio e Pepe Soup

Preparation: 10 minutes **Cooking:** 15 minutes **Servings:** 2 generous

Ingredients:
5 zucchini
3 eggs
1 cup grated cheese Cacio, or Grana Padano
1 chopped shallot
2 tablespoons extra virgin olive oil
A pinch of salt
A sprinkling of black pepper
1 ladle of vegetable stock
8-10 leaves of chopped basil
½ cup dry white wine

Directions: Start by heating up a pot over medium heat and adding the olive oil. Once the oil is hot, add the chopped shallot and sauté until it becomes translucent. Add the zucchini to the pot and continue to cook until they begin to soften, about 5-7 minutes. Add the white wine to the pot and let it cook for a few minutes to allow the alcohol to evaporate. Pour in the vegetable stock and bring the mixture to a boil. Reduce the heat to a simmer and let it cook for 20 minutes or until the zucchini is fully cooked. In another bowl, whisk together the eggs, grated cheese, and a pinch of salt and pepper. Slowly pour the egg mixture into the pot, stirring constantly to prevent the eggs from clumping together. Once the eggs have fully cooked and the soup has thickened, turn off the heat and stir in the chopped basil. Serve the soup garnished with a sprinkle of black pepper and a drizzle of olive oil.

Nutrition per serving: calories 616, carbohydrates 21.7g, fat 41.85g, protein 24.45g

Potato Lamb and Olive Stew Preparation

Preparation time: 20 minutes **Cooking time:** 1 hours 45 minutes **Servings:** 10

Ingredients:
4 tablespoons almond flour
¾ cup low sodium chicken stock
1¼ pounds (567 g) small potatoes, halved
3 cloves garlic, minced
4 large shallots, cut into ½inch wedges
3 sprigs fresh rosemary
1tablespoon lemon zest
Coarse sea salt and black pepper
3½ pounds (1.6 kg) lamb shanks, fat trimmed and cut crosswise into 1½ inch pieces
2 tablespoons extra virgin olive oil
½ cup dry white wine
1 cup pitted green olives, halved
2 tablespoons lemon juice

Directions: Preheat your oven to 400°F (200°C). In a small bowl, mix together the almond flour and chicken stock until smooth. In a large roasting pan, toss together the potatoes, garlic, shallots, rosemary, lemon zest, and a pinch of salt and pepper. Place the lamb shanks on top of the vegetables. Brush the lamb with the almond flour mixture and drizzle with the olive oil. Roast the lamb and vegetables in the preheated oven for 30 minutes. Reduce the heat to 350°F (180°C) and continue roasting for an additional 1 hour and 15 minutes, or until the lamb is tender and the vegetables are caramelized.

Remove the roasting pan from the oven and add the white wine, olives, and lemon juice. Stir to combine and let the stew sit for 5 minutes to allow the flavors to meld. Serve the stew hot, garnished with chopped fresh herbs if desired.

Nutrition: calories: 309, fat: 10.3g, protein: 36.9g, carbs: 16.1g, fiber: 2.2g, sodium: 239mg.

Pecorino Basil tomato Soup

Servings:4 **Cooking Time**: 65 Minutes

Ingredients:
½ cup Pecorino cheese, grated
2 tbsp olive oil
2 lb tomatoes, halved
2 garlic cloves, minced
1 onion, chopped
Salt and black pepper to taste
4 cups chicken stock
½ tsp red pepper flakes
½ cup basil, chopped

Directions: Preheat your oven to 400°F (200°C). Place the halved tomatoes, cut side up, on a baking sheet. Drizzle with 1 tbsp of the olive oil and sprinkle with salt and black pepper. Roast the tomatoes for 30-35 minutes, or until they are softened and slightly caramelized. In a large pot, heat the remaining 1 tbsp of olive oil over medium heat. Add the minced garlic and chopped onion, and cook until the onion is translucent, about 5-7 minutes. Add the roasted tomatoes, chicken stock, and red pepper flakes to the pot. Bring the mixture to a boil, then reduce the heat to low and let it simmer for 20-25 minutes. Use an immersion blender to blend the soup until it reaches your desired consistency (you can also transfer the soup to a blender, but be careful as it will be hot). Stir in the chopped basil and grated Pecorino cheese. Serve the soup hot, garnished with additional cheese and basil if desired.

Nutrition per serving: Calories: 240; Fat: 11g; Protein: 8g; Carbs: 16g.

Anchovy Fillet Halibut Stew

Prep time: 25 minutes **Cook time:** 30 minutes **Serving:** 1

Ingredients:
3 cups cherry tomatoes, halved
1 cup clam juice
4 tablespoons olive oil, divided
¼ cup sliced green onions
4 cloves garlic, sliced
1 anchovy fillet
2 pinches red pepper flakes
12 ounces halibut
1 pound shrimp
salt to taste
1 tablespoon chopped fresh parsley
½ tablespoon chopped fresh basil
½ tablespoon chopped fresh oregano
1 pinch minced fresh rosemary

Directions: Heat 2 tablespoons of olive oil in a large pot over medium heat. Add the green onions, garlic, anchovy fillet, and red pepper flakes. Sauté until the onions are soft and the anchovy fillet has dissolved. Add the halibut and shrimp to the pot and cook until they are no longer pink. Add the cherry tomatoes, clam juice, and enough water to cover the ingredients. Bring to a boil, then reduce the heat to a simmer. In a separate pan, heat the remaining 2 tablespoons of olive oil over medium heat. Add the parsley, basil, oregano, and rosemary. Sauté for 1 minute. Add the herb mixture to the pot with the halibut and shrimp. Season with salt to taste. Simmer the stew for 20 minutes, or until the vegetables are tender. Serve hot, garnished with additional chopped herbs if desired.

Nutrition: Calories: 681, Fat: 45g, Saturated fat: 7g, Cholesterol: 315mg, Sodium: 891mg, Carbohydrates: 25g, Fiber: 4g, Sugar: 14g, Protein: 46g

Butternut Squash and Cauliflower Soup

Preparation time: 10 minutes **Cooking time:** 45 minutes **Servings:** 4 to 6

Ingredients:
1 pound (454 g) butternut squash, peeled and cut into 1-inch cubes
1 small head cauliflower, cut into 1,5-inch pieces
1 onion, sliced
2 tablespoons coconut oil
1 tablespoon currypowder
½ cup no-added-sugar apple juice
4 cups low-sodium vegetable soup
2 tablespoons coconut oil
1 teaspoon sea salt
¼ teaspoon freshly ground white pepper
¼ cup chopped fresh cilantro, divided

Directions: Preheat your oven to 425°F (220°C). Spread the butternut squash and cauliflower out on a baking sheet. Drizzle with 1 tablespoon of coconut oil and sprinkle with curry powder. Toss to coat evenly. Roast the vegetables in the preheated oven for 20-25 minutes, or until tender. In a large pot, heat the remaining 1 tablespoon of coconut oil over medium heat. Add the onion and cook until it's soft and translucent, about 5 minutes. Add the roasted vegetables to the pot, along with the apple juice and vegetable soup. Bring the mixture to a boil, then reduce the heat to low and simmer for 10 minutes. Using an immersion blender, puree the soup until it's smooth and creamy. Alternatively, you can transfer the soup to a blender and blend until smooth, working in batches if necessary. Season the soup with salt and white pepper, then stir in half of the chopped cilantro. Serve the soup hot, garnished with the remaining cilantro.

Nutrition: calories: 415, fat: 30.8g, protein: 10.1g, carbs: 29.9g, fiber: 7.0g, sodium: 1386mg

CONCLUSION

One of the most complete beginner's Mediterranean cookbooks is this one. The recipes are simple to follow and include helpful Directions, so they are perfect for anyone learning to cook or simply interested in learning more about this cuisine.

A beginner's guide to the Mediterranean diet! This special cookbook teaches readers how to swap out conventionally unhealthy meals for healthier ones that are equally delicious. The Mediterranean diet does not emphasize eating a lot of fruits and vegetables every day. People can easily become overwhelmed by all the meals that need to be prepared if they even begin! Readers can choose a recipe from the large variety available based on their interests and preferences. Additionally, readers have the option to create individual dishes. While some readers might choose to prepare Mediterranean style soups, others might love cooking pasta dishes with a Mediterranean influence. They can decide!

The Mediterranean diet places a greater focus on plant foods than many other diets do. Whole grains, vegetables, and legumes frequently make up the bulk or a sizeable component of a meal. These foods are often made using a lot of flavorful spices and healthy fats like olive oil. Trace amounts of fish, meat, or eggs can be found in several dishes. Popular drinks include sparkling water, still water, and plain water; small amounts of red wine are also acceptable.

A diet that is high in natural foods, such as whole grains, vegetables, and healthy fats, is generally something that one should aim for. Anyone who is unhappy with their diet should consult a nutritionist for help. They will offer more or different foods that will help increase satiety. As was already noted, the Mediterranean diet encourages you to eat whatever you can enjoy at the table rather than restricting your intake as is the case with many other diets. This makes it a very flexible diet that gives you the chance to eat foods that are both healthy and delicious and to take care of your fitness so that your whole wellbeing is implemented as appropriate.

You can enjoy all the advantages that this diet has to offer for both you and the people you care about as long as you follow these straightforward principles. You will notice a difference in your general health as soon as you begin incorporating the recipes in this book.

By gradually incorporating the Mediterranean dishes in this book into your life, you'll not only be able to reap its many advantages without giving up flavor or other dining pleasures, but you'll also be able to wow your visitors.

12 WEEK MEAL PLAN

B. Breakfast **L.** Lunch **D.** Dinner

	Sunday	Monday	Tuesday	Wednesday	Thursday	Friday	Saturday
WEEK 1	**B.** Pancakes with Berry Sauce	**B.** Bulgur Breakfast Bowls	**B.** Broccoli and Eggs	**B.** Nectarine bruschetta	**B.** Strawberry Thyme Millet Bowl	**B.** Scrambled Egg Tacos	**B.** Hazelnuts, Blueberries Salad
	L. Mediterranean Salad	**L.** Baked Pangrattato Lamb	**L.** Pasta with pine nuts	**L.** Lemony Shrimp and Risotto	**L.** Roasted Vegetable	**L.** Salmon Pasta	**L.** Shrimp Scampi and Pasta
	D. Beef Stew with Eggplants	**D.** Pepper Meat	**D.** Lamb Stew	**D.** Beef Shanks	**D.** Spinach and Artichoke Frittata	**D.** Red Lentils Stew	**D.** Smoked Salmon
WEEK 2	**B.** Savory Breakfast Oatmeal	**B.** Sautéed Dandelion Toast	**B.** Zucchini Breakfast Salad	**B.** Breakfast Kale Frittata	**B.** Ricotta, Tartine	**B.** Breakfast Corn Salad	**B.** Pancakes with Berry Sauce
	L. Melon Caprese Salad	**L.** Seafood Paella	**L.** Pasta primavera with shrimp	**L.** Pesto Pasta	**L.** Mediterranean Fish	**L.** Lemony Shrimp and Risotto	**L.** Risotto with Parmesan
	D. Mushroom and Potato Oat Burgers	**D.** Classic Roasted Chicken	**D.** Slow Cooker Beef	**D.** Spanish Chicken Skillet	**D.** Colorful Sardines Omelet	**D.** PanSeared Salmon and Asparagus	**D.** Mediterranean Chicken
WEEK 3	**B.** Banana quinoa	**B.** Carrots Breakfast Mix	**B.** Shakshuka	**B.** Fresh Fruits	**B.** Spinach Feta Breakfast	**B.** Breakfast Cauliflower Rice Bowl	**B.** Nectarine Bruschetta
	L. Pasta with pine nuts	**L.** Salmon Pasta	**L.** Mediterranean Salad	**L.** Slow Cooker Mediterranean Pasta	**L.** Baked Pangrattato Lamb	**L.** Shrimp Scampi and Pasta	**L.** Sicilian style linguine
	D. Mushroom and Potato Oat Burgers	**D.** Pepper Meat	**D.** Beef Stew with Eggplants	**D.** Beef Shanks	**D.** Smoked Salmon	**D.**	**D.** Spinach and Artichoke Frittata
WEEK 4	**B.** Warm Bulgur Breakfast Bowls with Fruits	**B.** Warm Bulgur Breakfast Bowls with Fruits	**B.** Broccoli and Eggs	**B.** Strawberry Bowl	**B.** Scrambled Egg Tacos	**B.** Breakfast Kale Frittata	**B.** Banana quinoa
	L. Pasta primavera with shrimp	**L.** Pesto Pasta	**L.** Melon Caprese Salad	**L.** Seafood Paella	**L.** Pasta with pine nuts	**L.** Risotto with Parmesan	**L.** Mediterranean Fish
	D. Lamb Stew	**D.** Colorful Sardines Omelet	**D.** Classic Roasted Chicken	**D.** Mushroom and Potato Oat Burgers	**D.** Slow Cooker Beef	**D.** Spanish Chicken Skillet	**D.** Pepper Meat

W E E K 5	**B.** Zucchini Breakfast Salad	**B.** Broccoli and Eggs	**B.** Breakfast Pancakes with Berry Sauce	**B.** Scrambled Egg Tacos	**B.** Hazelnuts Salad	**B.** Savory Breakfast Oatmeal	**B.** Sautéed Dandelion Toast
	L. Salmon Pasta	**L.** Lemony Shrimp and Risotto	**L.** Pasta with pine nuts	**L.** Shrimp Scampi and Pasta	**L.** Baked Pangrattato Lamb	**L.** Seafood Paella	**L.** Mediterranean Fish
	D. Red Lentils Stew	**D.** Spinach and Artichoke Frittata	**D.** Pork Loin	**D.** Pan Seared Salmon and Asparagus	**D.** Mushroom and Potato Oat Burgers	**D.** Beef Stew with Eggplants	**D.** Smoked Salmon
W E E K 6	**B.** Breakfast Pancakes with Berry Sauce	**B.** Scrambled Egg Tacos	**B.** Strawberry Thyme Millet Bowl	**B.** Hazelnuts Salad	**B.** Ricotta,Egg Fried Tartine	**B.** Zucchini Breakfast Salad	**B.** Banana quinoa
	L. Sicilian style linguine	**L.** Pesto Pasta	**L.** Slow Cooker Mediterranean Pasta	**L.** Mediterranean Salad	**L.** Shrimp Scampi and Pasta	**L.** Risotto with Parmesan	**L.** Pasta primavera with shrimp
	D. Slow Cooker Beef	**D.** Pepper Meat	**D.** Red Lentils Stew	**D.** Colorful Sardines Omelet	**D.** Lamb Stew	**D.** Classic Roasted Chicken	**D.** Mushroom and Potato Oat Burgers
W E E K 7	**B.** Scrambled Egg Tacos	**B.** Broccoli and Eggs	**B.** Spinach Feta Breakfast	**B.** Sautéed Dandelion Toast	**B.** Savory Breakfast Oatmeal	**B.** Fresh Fruits	**B.** Breakfast Cauliflower
	L. Seafood Paella	**L.** Baked Pangrattato Lamb	**L.** Melon Caprese Salad	**L.** Salmon Pasta	**L.** Pasta with pine nuts	**L.** Lemony Shrimp and Risotto	**L.** Baked Pangrattato Lamb
	D. Mussels and Clams	**D.** Beef Stew with Eggplants	**D.** Smoked Salmon	**D.** Spinach and Artichoke Frittata	**D.** Mushroom and Potato Oat Burgers	**D.** Spanish Chicken Skillet	**D.** Red Lentils Stew
W E E K 8	**B.** Breakfast Pancakes with Berry Sauce	**B.** Banana quinoa	**B.** Zucchini Breakfast Salad	**B.** Strawberry Thyme Millet Bowl	**B.** Ricotta, Egg Fried Tartine	**B.** Breakfast Cauliflower	**B.** Fresh Fruits
	L. Risotto with Parmesan	**L.** Shrimp Scampi and Pasta	**L.** Mediterranean Salad	**L.** Pesto Pasta	**L.** Mediterranean Fish	**L.** Slow Cooker Pasta	**L.** Sicilianstyle linguine
	D. Slow Cooker Beef	**D.** Lamb Stew	**D.** Classic Roasted Chicken	**D.** Colorful Sardines Omelet	**D.** Pork Loin	**D.** Red Lentils Stew	**D.** Pepper Meat
W E E K 9	**B.** Hazelnuts Salad	**B.** Fresh Fruits	**B.** Sautéed Dandelion Toast	**B.** Broccoli and Eggs	**B.** Savory Breakfast Oatmeal	**B.** Breakfast Cauliflower	**B.** Scrambled Egg Tacos
	L. Salmon Pasta	**L.** Pasta with pine nuts	**L.** Baked Pangrattato Lamb	**L.** Lemony Shrimp and Risotto	**L.** Seafood Paella	**L.** Slow Cooker Mediterranean Pasta	**L.** Pasta primavera with shrimp
	D. Spinach and Artichoke Frittata	**D.** Mushroom and Potato Oat Burgers	**D.** Spanish Chicken Skillet	**D.** Mussels and Clams	**D.** Beef Stew with Eggplants	**D.** Smoked Salmon	**D.** Slow Cooker Beef

W E E K 1 0	**B.** Sautéed Dandelion Toast	**B.** Zucchini Breakfast Salad	**B.** Hazelnuts Salad	**B.** Breakfast Pancakes with Berry Sauce	**B.** Strawberry Thyme Millet Bowl	**B.** Zucchini Breakfast Salad	**B.** Fresh Fruits
	L. Mediterranean Fish	**L.** Mediterranean Salad	**L.** Slow Cooker Mediterranean Pasta	**L.** Seafood Paella	**L.** Melon Caprese Salad	**L.** Pesto Pasta	**L.** Risotto with Parmesan
	D. Colorful Sardines Omelet	**D.** Red Lentils Stew	**D.** Pepper Meat	**D.** Shrimp Scampi and Pasta	**D.** Lamb Stew	**D.** Classic Roasted Chicken	**D.** Pork Loin
W E E K 1 1	**B.** Banana quinoa	**B.** Ricotta, Egg Fried Tartine	**B.** Broccoli and Eggs	**B.** Zucchini Breakfast Salad	**B.** Scrambled Egg Tacos	**B.** Savory Breakfast Oatmeal	**B.** Sautéed Dandelion Toast
	L. Seafood Paella	**L.** Salmon Pasta	**L.** Pasta with pine nuts	**L.** Lemony Shrimp and Risotto	**L.** Baked Pangrattato Lamb	**L.** Sausage & Pasta	**L.** Pasta primavera with shrimp
	D. Red Lentils Stew	**D.** Beef Stew with Eggplants	**D.** Mussels and Clams	**D.** Spinach and Artichoke Frittata	**D.** Smoked Salmon	**D.** Shrimps in Tomato Sauce	**D.** Mediterranean Chicken
W E E K 1 2	**B.** Zucchini Breakfast Salad	**B.** Breakfast Pancakes with Berry Sauce	**B.** Hazelnuts Salad	**B.** Strawberry Thyme Millet Bowl	**B.** Spinach Feta Breakfast	**B.** Yogurt with dark chocolate flakes and almonds	**B.** Fresh Fruits
	L. Melon Caprese Salad	**L.** Slow Cooker Mediterranean Pasta	**L.** Baked Pangrattato Lamb	**L.** Pasta with pine nuts	**L.** Salmon Pasta	**L.** Mediterranean Salad	**L.** Lemony Shrimp and Risotto
	D. Classic Roasted Chicken	**D.** Pepper Meat	**D.** Red Lentils Stew	**D.** Shrimps in Tomato Sauce	**D.** Pork Loin	**D.** Colorful Sardines Omelet	**D.** Mushroom and Potato Oat Burgers

Made in the USA
Monee, IL
28 May 2023

34833727R00057